Pride, Faith, and Fear

Pride, Faith, and Fear

Islam in Sub-Saharan Africa

Charlotte A. Quinn and Frederick Quinn

OXFORD
UNIVERSITY PRESS
2003

OXFORD
UNIVERSITY PRESS

Oxford   New York
Auckland   Bangkok   Buenos Aires   Cape Town   Chennai
Dar es Salaam   Delhi   Hong Kong   Istanbul   Karachi   Kolkata
Kuala Lumpur   Madrid   Melbourne   Mexico City   Mumbai
Nairobi   São Paulo   Shanghai   Taipei   Tokyo   Toronto

Copyright © 2003 by Charlotte A. Quinn and Frederick Quinn

Published by Oxford University Press, Inc.
198 Madison Avenue, New York, New York 10016

www.oup.com

Library of Congress Cataloging-in-Publication Data
Quinn, Charlotte A.
Pride, faith, and fear : Islam in Sub-Saharan Africa / Charlotte A. Quinn and Frederick
Quinn.
    p. cm.
Includes bibliographical references and index.
ISBN 0-19-506386-4
1. Islam—Africa, Sub-Saharan—History—20th century.   2. Islam and state—Africa,
Sub-Saharan.   3. Religion and state—Africa, Sub-Saharan.   4. Africa,
Sub-Saharan—Religion.I. Quinn, Frederick.   II. Title.
BP64.A37 Q56 2002
297'.0967—dc21   2002019044

9 8 7 6 5 4 3 2 1

Printed in the United States of America
on acid-free paper

Acknowledgments

Charlotte A. Quinn had been working on this book for more than 20 years at her untimely death on June 17, 2000. She was long interested in Africa, and her senior research project at Bryn Mawr College in 1956 was on the independence of Ghana; in 1970 she received one of the first doctorates in African history awarded at the University of California at Los Angeles. Her thesis, *Mandingo Kingdoms of the Senegambia*, a study on the interaction of African and European societies based on oral interviews in the Senegambia, French, and British archival sources, was published in book form by Northwestern University Press in 1972.

Much of the present work was in manuscript form at the time of her death. Charlotte had written the Nigeria section after we had returned from two months in Abuja in May 2000, her fourth such research trip to Africa. She had prepared the sections on the Sudan and Senegal as well. I wrote the chapters on East and South Africa, regions we had visited together, and Charlotte had drafted most of the introduction, to which I added the concluding pages on Islamism, excerpted from a talk she gave at the Department of State's Foreign Service Institute to diplomats assigned to Africa. Beyond that, my principal task was to update information on personalities and movements within African Islam.

Professor John O. Voll, professor of Islamic history at Georgetown University's Center for Muslim-Christian Understanding provided valuable counsel, as did Cynthia Read of Oxford University Press. Dr. Pauline Baker, a friend of Charlotte and of me, offered encouragement at an important stage. Moussa Shitu, protocol assistant at the American Embassy, Abuja, was a generous host in Nigeria. Cheikh Anta Mbacke Babou of Michigan State University commented on the draft Senegal chapter, as did Ambassador Arye Oded on the section on Kenya. Ebrahim Moosa and Muhammad Haron shared insights on Islam in South Africa. Peter von Sievers, Bernard Weiss, Hakan Yavuz, and Ibrahim Karawan of the University of Utah History Department and Middle East Center were generous with their time and comments.

Charlotte had lived in Dakar, Senegal, as a student and in Yaounde, Cameroon, as a Foreign Service wife. She had lectured on African history and wrote extensively about it in professional journals. Trained as a writer (she had been on the staff of *Life* magazine in its golden era) and as a historian who studied Hausa and social anthropology, she had a sensitive appreciation of the religious dimension of Islam and supported the efforts of Washington National Cathedral to promote an interfaith dialogue. The words of the Swahili poet Sayyid Abdallah (d. 1810) on the finality of death come to mind in recalling her own sudden death:

> Hear the meaning when I speak to you:
> Life resembles a lamp-flame in the wind;
> It cannot be stopped when it goes out;
> One moment one sees it, then it has gone out.
>
> Or it resembles a roaring fire,
> In a clearing, in the bushes;
> There descends a cloudful of rain in the woods,
> And it is extinguished; you could not blow it into life again.[1]

Contents

Pride, Faith, and Fear

Introduction

African Islam: A Complex Reality

The history of Islam in sub-Saharan Africa is one of slow diffusion through commercial arteries over centuries, interspersed with brief paroxysms of activity, which has left a large segment of the population observing the five pillars of belief and Muslim communities facing widely different political and social conditions. As a result, these communities are different yet retain strong similarities. This book focuses on Muslims living in the Sudanic belt south of the Sahara, on the eastern coast facing the Indian Ocean, and in the far south of Africa, regions that encompass a wide variety of political situations. This is where you will find

- Large Muslim populations contesting predominantly Christian or animist groups for political leadership—as in Nigeria, where despite the community's size, internal divisions prevent a sense of common identity among ethnic groups and generations
- A westernized majority Muslim population politically on top but facing acute economic challenges and generational tensions—in Senegal
- A Muslim-run government with tenuous claims to legitimacy that has fought a costly civil war since 1989, has imposed a strict Islamic government on a religiously diverse population, but has

failed to override long-established North-South Arab and African divisions—in Sudan

- Coastal, urbanized Arab minorities receptive to a secessionist option and resentful of political control by Christian, non-Muslim governments in the interior—as in Kenya
- A small (less than 2% of the population) Islamic community ethnically and ideologically divided, sandwiched between larger white and black populations, and seeking its identity in the harsh aftermath of apartheid—in South Africa.

As Africa enters a new millennium, it faces few prospects of satisfying its populations' desires for social or economic stability, let alone prosperity. All over Africa, converts to Islam seek assurances that in this world or the next they will be on the winning side, that God will reward them either here or in the hereafter. Meanwhile, to honor their religion they assert the need to observe Muslim duties in all facets of life; state after state, in Nigeria, for example, is passing legislation that institutes the Sharia as law, in some cases realizing after the fact that they were not sure what they have passed and how to go about observing it.

This book addresses two problems characteristic of attitudes and knowledge of Islam in the West—and by extension of impressions flowing the other way. All too often the Muslim world is treated as having a single dimension, as if Muslims in general had bonded with Osama bin Laden. Similarly, many Muslims hold stubbornly to the idea that Christians have not abandoned the Crusaders' mentality, zealously trying to destroy all traces of Muslim civilizations in their entirety. Old images loom large, and they influence contemporary analysis. Consider the portrayal of Arabs in much Western art, scheming sensualists with hooded eyes and cunning smiles, ready to plunge scimitars into white soldiers and to rape their women. Variations of this Orientalist theme appear in innumerable canvasses of French nineteenth-century artists and in popular British magazine fiction, and today they are as close as the latest TV or film portrayal of Arabs. A study of how Arabs were depicted in 900 films was reported by Jack G. Shaheen, whose "Worst List" included *Rules of Engagement*, based on a story by a former secretary of the navy, James Webb. It depicts Arab women and children killing Americans in Yemen. A critic has written, "Arabs have always had the roughest and most uncomprehending deal from Hollywood, but with the death of the cold war the stereotype has been granted even more wretched prominence."[1]

Muslims fare no better in popular history or on the pages of foreign policy briefings. Many are assumed to be fundamentalists, ignorant of the

West, for whom terrorism is an acceptable course of action. But histori-cally, African Islam was tolerant and diverse. Peter von Sievers draws a telling picture of Egypt. Egyptian Islam was historically urbane and univ-ersalist (now called "globalist") in outlook from its inception until after World War II. But rigid Islamists, an outgrowth of the Muslim Brother-hood (founded in 1928), found easy prey in growing unemployment among young people and poor economic conditions. "Nationalism and socialism were condemned as godless Western ideologies. . . . Mysticism was denigrated as a relic of the past," and expressions of moderate Sunni orthodoxy became the targets of small groups of terrorists.[2] Yet for many westerners, it was the headline-grabbing extremists who were thought to be the dominant voices of contemporary Islam.

Perceptions of the West are equally skewed among African Muslims. Although many Muslims are eager to incorporate aspects of Western ma-terial culture into their lifestyle, there is a pervasive belief among African Muslims that the West is on a new crusade against Islam. When the young Turkish assassin attempted to shoot the pope on May 13, 1981, he de-clared, "I have decided to kill Pope John Paul II, supreme commander of the Crusades."[3] This is a perception that is likely to color the outlook of future leaders of the Muslim community, whether they are traditionalist or Islamist. This charge is being leveled in the wake of the suppression of the Front Islamique du Salut (FIS) in Algeria, the rocky state of the Middle East peace process, and even in the plight of Kosovo Muslims. The fact that the last became victims of ethnic cleansing by Christian Serbs and were expelled from their lands after the West took up their cause has seemed to prove a point for some African Muslims.

Ironically, the same Muslim groups that denounce Western influences in Africa may do so by cassette tapes, cellular phones, fax machines, and Internet websites. And one member of a Muslim group may inveigh against the global capitalistic economy while others seek visas to work in France, Germany, or the United States.

A distinct characteristic of Islam in Africa is that patience is running out among marginalized people, many of whom want to remove the sources of political and economic oppression they face, as well as corrup-tion in government and the threat of Western secularism. Over the past 20 years, many Muslims in northern Nigeria have focused their reformist zeal locally on contradictions and impurities in Islamic practices, a strug-gle that has characterized Islamic reform throughout the world for cen-turies. Also, the removal of the harsh hand of military dictatorship has encouraged many believers to frame their expressions of despair over con-tinuing social and economic inequities in religious terms.

Most African Muslims would not approve of the terrorist bombings in New York City and Washington on September 11, 2001, and would regard them as the work of extremists from whom they disassociate themselves. Notwithstanding, a driven minority will support the bombings, believing that somehow their lot will be better if a blow is struck at materialistic (World Trade Center) and militant (Pentagon) America. Neither reason nor compassion informs such a position, but reason and compassion are not the properties of desperate people. It is among such people that extremists will find a willing or at least an acceptable climate for terrorism and disruption.

Islam's Growing Numbers: 150 Million to 160 Million African Muslims

Nearly one in every five persons in the world is Muslim, and Islam is spreading more rapidly in sub-Saharan Africa than any other religion, despite the vigorous efforts of Christian missionaries. Both Christian and Muslim proselytizers feed off the remains of rapidly diminishing traditional religious communities. The growth of Islamic numbers in Africa is due to conversions but possibly even more to the rapid expansion of populations that are already Muslim. Within the past 15 years, estimates of the size of the African Muslim community have grown from 120 million to between 150 million and 160 million—over 30% of sub-Saharan Africa's total population. In East Africa, over 40% of the population, some 60 million individuals, are Muslim. In West Africa, there are over 80 million Muslims. In Nigeria alone, Muslims are estimated to number some 58 million. (In 1963, the date of the last official census, Nigeria's Muslim population was 26 million.) Southern Africa has some 4 million Muslims.

At this point, virtually every African country has at least a small Muslim community, ranging in size from a few thousand in Zimbabwe to virtually the entire population of Somalia and Senegal. A majority of the population in Guinea, Mali, and the Niger Republic are Muslim. The remaining third of Africa's Muslim population is found in Northeast, East, and Central Africa. One hundred percent of the population of Zanzibar and Somali is Muslim, as are one-fourth to one-third of the populations of Ethiopia, Eritrea, Mozambique, and Tanzania. Thus, the total of sub-Saharan African Muslims is roughly the equivalent of the total found in North Africa.[4]

Other demographic trends will also alter these African Muslim communities during the next 10 years. The mass movement of African youths from impoverished rural communities into cities in search of jobs will create large dislocated populations of "foot soldiers," available for extremist causes that flourish in such urban settings. These unemployed young people, mostly males in the 16- to 30-year-old range, resemble the *hittistes* of Algeria, "those who prop up the walls." Haunting city streets, bus stations, and market squares in search of work and amusement, these uprooted young people are easily recruited by offers of food, shelter, and access to some form of employment. In Nigeria, the Maitatsine—a movement that introduced Islamic innovations and rejected Western consumer culture and was disavowed by mainstream Muslims—has recruited tens of thousands of youths in this fashion. An active Muslim Brotherhood (a Nigerian version without institutional ties to the organization of the same name in Egypt and Sudan) attracted large numbers of followers in Nigeria's northern and central states by using similar recruitment techniques. As youthful populations grow in the cities, traditional faith communities and social structures of family, kinship, and local political life will weaken.

In the studies that follow we will consider the contemporary "look" of several national Muslim communities—who they are and their origins—and the contemporary political scene in the states where they are found. In the process, national Islamic institutions, beliefs, and leadership will be considered. We will analyze the political issues involved in Islam's survival and growth and its interactions with other groups within the society and emphasize the changing, contradictory, and emergent nature of Islamic civilization.

This book is written more for a broad audience than a scholarly one. It explains Islam's attraction for an increasing number of converts and indicates the stabilizing, as well as destabilizing, impact of the spread of Islam in African societies. It emphasizes the variety of local Islamic manifestations and the importance of the north-south divide along the east-west axis of the Sahara desert, as well as the political implications of the contrast between Sufi and reformist beliefs and generational changes that pose important challenges to leadership within the communities.

African Islam: Local and Global

African Islam is first of all local Islam. There is no Islamic pope or curia, no ordained clergy, and no international body to regulate doctrine. Since there are no specific educational or doctrinal standards beyond adherence to the five basic tenants of Islam, there is considerable variety within the preaching and practices of individual mosques throughout the continent.

The primary faith community is composed of individuals gathered around separate mosques whose worship leaders are generally raised up from the local community and speak a local language, possibly Arabic as well. The local focus of African Islam contributes to its inability to organize effectively beyond local units. Individual mosque leaders focus their energies on single congregations and only rarely form into larger groups. Kenneth Cragg, Anglican bishop and student of Islam, has described the local orientation of Islamic worship: "There is no priesthood, no bewildering incantation, no solemn music, no curtained mysteries, no garments for sacred wear contrasted with those of the street and marketplace. All proceeds within a congregational unison in which the imam, or leader, does no more than occupy the space before the niche and set the time for the sequence of movements in which all participate."[5]

African Islam is also global in scope, with its members tracking issues that affect Muslims in the Middle East, Asia, Bosnia, and the United States. Modern communications technology feeds such an informational flow, as does easy air access to Mecca, Cairo, and elsewhere. African Muslims' understanding of life abroad is augmented by the millions of Muslims who are migrating to Western countries. Islam has become the fastest growing religion in the United States, with over 5 million Muslims already. In Europe, there are some 5 million in France and highly visible populations in Britain and Germany.[6]

What is missing between these two worlds, the local and the global, is any kind of organization that bridges them. A few national councils exist on paper, but their performance records are not strong, and there is no effectual wider Islamic presence, no all-African Muslim council. This means that looking at African Islam is like looking at a prism (an often-employed Islamic image), with endless combinations emanating from its colors and forms, a whole being is projected, but one that takes its distinctive traits from an inexhaustible range of parts.

Moreover, Islam is an imported religion in much of Africa, overlaid on local belief systems, which provided their own explanations about life and death, how to deal with reversals and good fortune, and how to make peace with the forces that govern the universe. What often happened was that elements of folk belief, ritual, and music were retained and given an Islamic overlay. Thus the blending of Islamic and pre-Islamic cultures was a distinctive feature of Islam in Africa, to which the prayers of Sufi mystics and the language of the Koran was added. Arabic, it will be remembered, was a foreign language in much of Africa.

It is difficult to overstate the importance of Islam as a source of identity to Africans in societies that are experiencing rapid change. To be able to say, "I am a Muslim" is to have an identity and access to a wider community of shared beliefs, a code of behavior in the present world, and hope for the life hereafter. Believers can gain strength from the knowledge that they are part of a worldwide community (*umma*). They can also, within a village or town, establish a distinct identity by declaring themselves part of a wider community of Islam. For such believers Islam represents "a system of ideas, informal networks of scholars and saints, organized around the messages of the Koran, building a righteous social order; in short, a system of symbolic interaction."[7] Such prospects comfort in the best of times, more so in a world where hopes of economic advancement are lacking, corruption is rampant, and the older, more settled ways of life are under attack. In such a setting, to hear the daily call to prayer is to hear a call to a life of meaning and purpose. Conversely, to define and stand against the ignorant or the heretics (*jahiliyya*) contributes to Muslim identity, especially among militant members.

Muslim identity in Africa does not mean primarily individual identity, as it might in the West, but the collective identity of a person or persons in a wider social context. Thus a Muslim in Nigeria, Sudan, Senegal, Kenya, or South Africa would consider oneself part of both a nuclear family and an extended family and of an ethnic and linguistic group as well. Most often, the language, in addition to English and French, would be a local one, such as Wolof, Hausa, or Swahili. Some African Muslims would also speak and write Arabic, for the debate over whether or not public prayers and sermons should be conducted in Arabic or in a local language is a lively one.

In the West, a statement that identifies a person as a member of a nation-state, such as "I am an American" or "I am a citizen of Great Britain," would be an important part of a person's identity. This would be true of African Muslims as well, but with an important qualification. For many African Muslims, their religious identity is more important than their national identity. For example, for many Nigerian Muslims, the state is a disappointment—corrupt, invertebrate, and nonfunctional; for Kenyan Muslims, the state, largely dominated by Christians, is both corrupt and discriminates against them. The state in Sudan is plagued by one of the world's longest and most costly civil wars, which is one reason reformist Muslims find their identity in a polity governed by Islamic law. In South Africa, the grim apartheid era has been replaced by independence, but with a governing body that is far from solving its internal public safety and security needs, giving rise to Muslim vigilante groups. In Senegal, membership in one of the major brotherhoods is at least as important as being a Senegalese citizen. Many African Muslims would agree with the conservative Indian Islamic cleric Kalim Siddiqui: "The greatest evil that stalks the modern world [is] nationalism. . . . These nation-states are like huge boulders blown across our path by the ill-wind of recent history. All nation-states that today occupy, enslave and exploit the lands, peoples and resources of the *umma* must of necessity be dismantled."[8]

An additional part of any group's identity is the way in which members look at their history, not as professional historians might but in the way that people combine myth and fact, telescope them together, and teach them to their children, outsiders, and the world as a statement of "who we are." In the case of African Muslims, such popular history begins with the question of origins. Nigerians and Senegalese can trace their histories to early Muslim kingdoms in North Africa and to heroes like Uthman Dan Fodio and El Hajj Umar. In Senegal, there is a hallowed past, to which are added the histories of leaders of brotherhoods, such as Amadou Bamba, founder of the Mouride brotherhood, and El Hajj Malick Sy, caliph of the Tijaniya brotherhood. Sudanese Muslims have ancient ties to Egypt and the Arabian Peninsula and to important figures like the Mahdi. The geographies of Kenya and South Africa have influenced the identity of Islam there, principally because of maritime influences, which provided an Islamic presence from overseas.

Moreover, the history of each Muslim community's relationship with colonialism helped give shape and definition to its identity. Although many African peoples profited through education, economic advantages, and improved health conditions, colonialism's negative aspects included new political boundaries that often disrupted traditional societies; a re-orientation of economies toward Europe rather than the Arab world; exposure to Western, secularist political, economic, and social ideas; and encounters with growing numbers of Christians, often in a hostile setting.[9]

And since Islam is a global religion, Muslim identity in Africa, at least in leadership classes, is cognizant of such events as the emergence of a strong, modern Islamic state in Egypt; the Israeli-Palestinian problem; the overthrow of the shah of Iran and the creation of an Islamic government under the Ayatollah Khomeini; and most recently, the events of September 11, 2001, and their aftermath. In such a view of history, there are both sources of pride (the 1956 defeat of the British and French forces at Suez and the Iranian revolution) and anger (the partition of the Arab world and of Africa by colonial powers and the failure of many modern, postindependence African states.)

Although reaction to key aspects of their history will differ among African Muslim communities, and the ground nut cultivator in Senegal will not have the same outlook as a university professor in Khartoum, the point is that the historical building blocks contributing to their identities are vastly different for Muslims in Africa than for people in the West. This is reflected in a popular interpretation of history, representing the distillation of myth and fact that is repeated in mosque sermons, read in publications, listened to on cassette tapes, and is available on radio and television and, most recently, on the Internet. Such history is selective and personal, inconsequential for many academics but extremely important in crafting a distinctive Islamic identity in Africa, one variously informing the actors in this story.

Sharia, the One Law

To devout Muslims, Sharia is the measure by which a society is judged to be Islamic, outweighing the numbers of pilgrims to Mecca, support of Islamic charities, and the other obligations of Islam. Yet the meaning of Sharia and how it should be implemented is by no means clear.

In countries lacking cohesion or creditable political structure, Sharia provides a way of life, as the Talmud did in ancient Israel and canon law did in the Christian Middle Ages. Not only does Sharia offer an equitable way to resolve commercial disputes and family issues, such as inheritance, but also it traces its wellsprings to the Prophet and the Koran and thus brings the whole of life under divine rule. In a pluralistic African setting, Sharia assumes a major importance for Muslims, representing the glue that holds society together.

The issue about how widely the Sharia can be applied continues to draw verbal fire from both Muslim and Christian communities. Christian leaders oppose any strengthening of Islamic law in Nigeria and the Sudan, and their Muslim counterparts predict chaos if it is neglected. In countries like Kenya and South Africa, with smaller Muslim populations, compromises allow Muslim personal law (MPL) to be introduced formally or informally, covering specific instances such as inheritance law. Across the spectrum, there are countries like Sudan, where proponents of Sharia want to make it a national law, while allowing exceptions for non-Muslim people; to countries like Nigeria, where bloody street battles are a prelude to efforts to make Sharia the law at the state level; to countries like Senegal and South Africa, where most Muslims are content to have parts of Sharia implemented.

With little economic relief in sight, Africa's Muslim populations, particularly those along the Islamic fringes of the Sahara and in the Horn of Africa, face intense pressure in finding ways to make ends meet. Continuing poverty is likely to increase political discontent, which will probably be expressed in faith-based political action in Muslim communities.

Nigeria has been dominated by Muslim-led national governments since it became independent of colonial rule. However, the northern Muslim community has suffered disproportionately from the Nigerian economy's virtual collapse because of its distance from coastal trade centers and its relative economic backwardness in relation to other regions of the country. Economic hardships will fuel Muslim discontent and encourage political radicalism unless the civilian government, elected in May 1999, addresses the North's problems effectively and soon.

The mass migration of Muslim youths to cities is contributing to a wave of criminal activity not only in Nigeria but also in Senegal, one of Africa's most stable democracies. Street crime has increased to the point that many Senegalese women are now afraid to wear their trademark gold jewelry outside the home.

As South Africa moves into the post-Mandela era, urban crime against the middle classes is taking tens of thousands of lives. The middle-class Muslim "Coloured" and Indian population is engaged in an increasingly politicized struggle to protect itself. Muslims have formed militias under the rubric "People against Gangsterism and Drugs (PAGAD)," which wage a violent battle against narcotic gangs in the region. The members of PAGAD have hostilely challenged the African National Congress (ANC) government as well because of its failure to protect the Muslim community. The PAGAD activists have mounted over 200 attacks on Western tourists, Muslim moderates, and the police in recent years, and PAGAD has joined forces with Qiblah—a small ultraradical Muslim group named for the mosque niche that points toward Mecca. Together, these groups are likely to press an Islamist agenda in the western Cape. Lacking numbers now, these groups still have the capacity to be a destabilizing force to South Africa's new democratic government.

The Christian presence in Africa will continue to grow in tandem with the spread of Islam, at the expense of traditional animist groups, over the next decade in virtually all of sub-Saharan Africa. Muslim competition with Christian activists for converts, economic benefits, and political power will sharpen Muslims' sense of identity and spark violent confrontations between the two communities within and across national boundaries. Chad, a key example of this clash, remains culturally and politically divided between an Islamic North and Christianized South, which fought each other in the 1960s. West African coastal states have yet to merge their Muslim northern districts with southern Christian and animist regions into a balanced political whole.

Both Christian and Muslim communities are growing in tandem throughout Africa. Their differences are likely to breed violence, particularly where they coincide with ethnic and geographic divides in both West and East Africa. Although these conflicts will unify some national Muslim communities by strengthening their sense of distinctive Muslim identity, other factors will continue to divide African Muslims and diminish their political influence. In particular, theological differences will embroil Muslim traditionalists and reform-minded Islamists as new generations challenge aging leaders and assert their right to Muslim community leadership. It is unlikely that a religious figure of the stature of Iran's Ayatollah Khomeini will emerge to unify Africa's Muslims, given the divisions within the Islamic community and the cultural constraints on political activism by Sunni clerics.

In Nigeria, communal disputes over membership in the Organization of Islamic Conference (OIC) and the constitutional status of the Sharia continue, despite efforts by domestic mediators to draw the two communities closer together. In 1999, Christian and Muslim leaders cooperated in a national coalition, allowing Nigeria to elect a democratic government. Both communities had suffered under General Abacha's rule, and less than a year before Nigeria appeared to be headed toward anarchy. Memories of the devastating effects of the Biafra war and fears of a return to ethnic-religious strife helped force the two communities to select two Christian candidates for head of state paired with northern Muslims for vice president. President Obasanjo was elected with the overwhelming support of northern Muslim constituencies as the first Yoruba Christian to take power from a northern Muslim chief executive.

However, the fault line between the two religious groups continues to divide many local communities in Nigeria and is likely to provoke violence, particularly if the economy fails to revive. It will be difficult to break out of a pattern of communal violence, which has been set over the past 20 years and has taken over 5,000 lives. Long after Obasanjo's election, Muslim-Christian violence has continued in the North.

In Sudan, conflicts between Muslims and Christians are waged in Africa's longest-running civil war between the Islamized Arab North and black, non-Muslim southern populations. The Bashir regime has adopted an official Islamist ideology and committed itself to a program of wholesale Islamization, enforcement of the Sharia, and pursuit of the long-standing conflict in the South through a jihad. The fighting has been most bitter since 1983, when the northerners imposed Islamic law on the entire country, including the Christian-animist South. The continuing military stalemate plus identification by both Christians and Muslims of their religious position in terms of nationalist ambitions make it unlikely that a single, multireligious state will emerge in the foreseeable future. The deep divisions underlying the Sharia conflict will probably continue even if accommodation on the religious issue is again brought to the bargaining table.

What becomes startlingly clear in talking with Muslim scholars and the rank and file is that the common heritage of Judaism, Christianity, and Islam forms a potentially workable religious alliance. The three world religions could make common cause to produce a world order that would answer the needs of the deprived masses of humanity. But such potential is unrealized, and sharp conflict ensues instead.

Sufism is still the strongest Islamic force in most of sub-Saharan Africa, despite the higher press profile of reformers. The Sufi brotherhoods (*tariqa*), centered on a religious leader and following his "path" of intense mysticism, will continue to play an important role in politics, as well as in popular religious belief and practice. Sufism is a mystical, ecstatic dimension of Islam. Through Sufi learning and practice, the individual seeks personal communion with God, usually under the guidance of a saintly master. (Sufis have been notably willing to accept traditional practices, such as the wearing of charms, and adapt them into Islamic practice.) Voll has correctly identified the brotherhoods as being important forces "for social cohesion and interregional unity," adding, "This great network of teachers and students provided one of the most important vehicles for the expansion of Islam in sub-Saharan Africa."[10] Several brotherhoods have expanded beyond national borders. Senegal's Tijaniya have a large following in northern Nigeria, and Mouridiya clerics follow peripatetic Wolof traders throughout West Africa, Europe, and North America.

In Senegal, where the Islamic community is highly organized by the Mouridiya, Tijaniya, and Qadiriya and their branches, the brotherhoods play an active part, exercising decisive political power behind the scenes and virtually controlling the economy. Future political stability in that country will be in large measure dependent on the maintenance of a careful balance between the brotherhoods' interests and the government. However, this balance could be upset in the future by the Mourides' economic success and growing political influence, which are already provoking resentment and retaliation from the other brotherhoods. Furthermore, with diminishing assets at its disposal, Senegal will be ill prepared in the future to meet Mourides' demands for a larger share of the land and other economic benefits.

The Sufi brotherhoods' future will largely depend on an ability to sustain their conservative institutions while offering an active program of "modernized" (Islamist) reform to new generations. In Sudan, the Khatmiya and Ansar brotherhoods held onto power throughout the colonial and postindependence periods, forming political parties only to be unseated by the Islamist Bashir regime. The search for a unifying principle has led many northern Sudanese leaders to advocate basing the political system on Islam, but Islamization will continue to create divisions between Muslims and non-Muslims and, within the Muslim community, between Islamists and more secular members. Thus for Sudan, Muslim politics are unlikely to overcome the country's basic instability. In Kenya, the brotherhoods are less influential than in neighboring Tanzania; in South Africa, they have even less influence than ethnic Islamic groups or followers of individual mosques.

Divided Aims, Diminished Influence

Many Muslim communities are likely to remain quiescent, particularly among the rural poor, who are generally politically passive and apolitical. Revival for these and for most Muslims represents a renewal of personal piety and a return to prescribed daily religious observance. In the Horn of Africa, where Muslims make up sizable percentages of the population, Islam remains only a minor player in the chronic instability that is derived from hostility between ethnic groups, border wars, and internal rebellions.

However, religious politics—both intra-Muslim and interfaith—will remain close to the surface in a number of West and East African countries. For a growing minority of urban Muslims, the Islamic revival involves political and social activism, as well as personal piety. In Kenya, for example, there is a deep ethnoreligious divide between the Muslim coastal and off-shore island population, settled by Middle Eastern Arabs, and the largely non-Muslim people on the mainland. With greater influence on the mainland government unlikely, the rise of Islamic consciousness on the coast and in the islands will fuel continuing unrest and desire for autonomy.

Although these issues—and Christian-Muslim rivalry—intensify feelings of Muslim unity, philosophical and tactical differences will continue to divide Islamic communities and retard the development of transnational religious movements that have political implications. Hasan al-Turabi, Sudan's principal Islamist leader, who has had aspirations for an international role, has met will little success in trying to establish effective transnational Muslim ties within Africa. Furthermore, the African Muslim community will find it difficult to overcome divisions created by postcolonial state borders and the legacy of multiple languages, which continue for the most part to prevent international organizations such as the OIC and Organization of African Unity (OAU) from achieving political relevance.

Over the next decade, African Muslims will continue to emerge from their historic isolation from the rest of the Muslim world. Taped and published sermons and political statements, promoting Islamic reform, delivered in Qom, Tripoli, Riyadh, Khartoum, or Jakarta are now readily available in the mosques and marketplaces of Kano, Durban, Dakar, and Dar-es-Salaam.

Organizations such as the OIC will continue to provide an international forum for Africa's Muslim minorities and channel limited assistance to them, although the collapse of oil prices since the 1970s oil boom has reduced levels of funding from the Middle East for African causes and institutions. State-supported organizations such as Libya's Islamic Call Society and Iranian and Libyan embassies and cultural centers will provide Islamist publications and education to a majority of African communities. Thousands of African students will study each year in the Middle East and North Africa and provide a recruiting ground for future Islamic activists.

Muslim leaders outside Africa, looking for political support in international organizations, will encourage these ties. High-level visits among Libya, Iran, and the Sudan and countries from Senegal to South Africa will continue to provide a measure of support to African governments and Muslim communities. The Saudi Arabian–funded mosque and Islamic center in N'Djamena, Chad; the Morocco-provided mosque in Conakry, Guinea; and the new mosque in Abuja, Nigeria, are three examples of buildings constructed on a grand scale and representing international Muslim ties.

Mu'ammar Qadhafi asserts that he feels more African than Arab because he is taken more seriously south of the Sahara than in the Arab world. Although many Africans are cynical about Qadhafi's dependability and trustworthiness after decades of experience, Libya continues to provide occasional economic aid and often supports African interests in international fora. Operating through the Islamic Call Society and a series of international organizations such as the Economic Community of Sahelian States (ECSS), as well as through personal contacts, Qadhafi continues to make high-profile political overtures to Libya's southern neighbors with some success. President Mandela has outspokenly praised Libyan support of the ANC during the struggle against apartheid and invited the Libyan leader, newly liberated from Western sanctions, to pay the last official visit of a foreign leader to South Africa during Mandela's presidency.

The pilgrimage is important in inoculating African Muslims with the concept of a world community to which they belong, a place to meet other Muslims, where experiences can be shared and beliefs affirmed. Each year the hajj brings thousands of faithful to the holy places and provides a rich forum for the exchange of ideas. For many, the pilgrimage is an opportunity to discover in the relaxed, almost casual surroundings of dormitory accommodations, the experiences of others in the African community.

These trends emphasize the attractions of a continent-wide Muslim community, and there is a striking visual impression of conformity to Muslim practices—mosques, people at prayer, and Islamic dress—throughout Africa. For the West, this sense of a worldwide community offers a rarely grasped opportunity to address Muslim concerns in Africa over a wide field. The American ambassador's words at the funerals of Kosovo victims of Serbia's ethnic cleansing put the United States in the forefront in condemning anti-Muslim violence. But, by the same token, actions perceived as hostile to Muslim interests in Israel, for example, resonate widely. America and the West are slow to seize the opportunity to engage African Islam in productive encounters.

Protean Islam: Roots (Ninth to Twentieth Centuries)

Islamic communities today represent the latest stage in a thousand-year continuum of Muslim experience, marked by a protean process of advance and decline that shapes the relationship of large numbers of Africans to one another and to the political authorities that control their lives. The roots of today's Islamic communities in Africa lie deep in the medieval development of a world Islamic community (*umma*), which stretched from Spain to China and south into the African savanna.[11] It was a bustling hive of travel, growing wealth, and the exchange of ideas. By the fourteenth century, when Africa's Sudanic states had been brought into this cosmopolitan world, Islamic civilization was at its height in the arts, sciences, law, and government.[12]

Islam traveled south of the Saharan barrier into what is now known as West Africa over many routes and by means of many agents. It entered the western Sudan as part of the spiritual baggage of Berber-Tuareg traders—veiled habitués of the desolate desert trade routes—who were seeking the fabled sources of gold, slaves, ivory, hides, and ostrich feathers in the upper reaches of the Niger and Senegal Rivers. Professional Muslim travelers and scholars from the Maghrib journeyed incessantly around Europe, Africa, and Asia from the ninth century on, joining trade caravans to visit the Sudanic kingdoms south over these trans-Saharan trade routes. By then, Arabs had made contact with ancient Ghana (1076), for which the modern state is named. Trade was the chief tie that linked Africa to the wider world and put it on the maps of the time.

For many years, contact focused on the courts of savanna rulers and foreign trading settlements. African rulers took advantage of Muslims' literacy, cosmopolitan experience, and far-reaching contacts to enhance trading networks and techniques of state building while continuing to observe pre-Islamic customs.

The further their rule extended, the greater the reach of Islamic law. Law held society together, and divine law both provided clear guidance about how a society should operate and connected it to its deepest wellsprings. With the establishment of Muslim schools and universities, a literate class of Muslim scholars, merchants, and administrators appeared. The literature of Arab scholarship was making its way into the region. Leo Africanus (c. 1465–1550) wrote an Arabic description of his travels in Africa, which was published in Italian in 1550. Based on his travels from Morocco to what is now northern Nigeria and Chad, he portrayed a land where active commerce and learning were widespread.[13]

Africans had already begun to make the hajj to the holy places in Arabia, bringing them to the attention of the wider world. Notable were the pilgrimages of Mansa Musa, followed by that of Askyia Mohammed (1495–1497), which fixed world attention on the western Sudan through the richness of their entourages and their dazzling expenditure of gold. After arduous travel, Askyia Mohammed found large states, controlling vast areas and many peoples of the western savanna and exploiting the resources of gold and ivory available there. Ibn Battuta, a fourteenth-century traveler and scholar who crossed the desert in 1352–1353, described what it was like to leave the cosmopolitan cities of northern Africa and verdant oases to arrive at the Sudanese empire of Mali. Though he was used to traveling throughout the world, he reported that he had "never seen anything more difficult" than segments of the rough road between Sijilmasa and Takadda, beset by fierce cold by night and burning heat during the day.

These early travelers laid the groundwork for the first great movement of Islamic revival in sub-Saharan Africa. According to the classic Arabian traveler, Ibn Khaldoun, the experience of a Berber chief on the hajj and the influence of a puritan Muslim cleric (Ibn Yasin) from Sijilmasa convinced him to undertake the purification of Islam in the region. The reformers, who met with little encouragement at first, were forced to withdraw to a fortified island monastery off the Atlantic coast—reinforcing the pattern set by the Prophet's withdrawal to Mecca from Medina, a pattern followed by militant nineteenth-century reformers in the Niger and Senegal valleys. From there, the Almoravids attacked Ghana and in 1062 destroyed its capital. Later scholars believe that the movement was not only the result of religious fervor but also a response to the pressure of Arab migration across North Africa and Ghana's demands for tribute from the south. In the end, all that the Almoravids accomplished was to destroy trade and agriculture in the region. Ghana reasserted its independence in a few years, though it never achieved control of the western savanna as before. Although their political and military successes were fleeting, the Almoravid conquest pushed forward the spread of Islam, and the rulers of Mali from the mid-thirteenth century were at least Muslim in name. The Almoravid conquest set the pattern for the ebb and flow of Islamization, of adaptive and reforming Islam, which remains a characteristic of African Muslim communities ever since.

The successor states that picked up the pieces of political authority left after the Almoravids shattered Ghana included Mali (1230), initially ruled by traditional animist leaders, and Gao (1464–1528), whose rulers found Islam useful in extending their control over large regions of the Sahel. These leaders believed that membership in a Muslim community formed a basis for loyalty beyond the ruler's family clan. At the same time, Muslim schools built an educated cadre of administrators to run the new imperial bureaucracy. Imposing Islamic law, they established benchmarks for peace and stability, which in turn encouraged trade and the enrichment of these large Sudanic states. Travelers were able to move freely, not needing guards and companions because of the safety of the road. Mosques were going up, and Islamic religious practice was meticulously observed in courts and royal towns. By the eleventh century, the kings of Kanem, far to the east and today located in what have become northern Nigeria and the Niger, had converted to Islam. Nevertheless, although Muslim kings ruled the Sudanic empires of the eleventh through the sixteenth centuries, it was only in the nineteenth century that the mass of the population began to convert to Islam, which until then had remained the domain of capitals and trading towns.

The difficulties of cross-Saharan travel protected these Sudanic states from many of the political consequences of Islam's spread westward across North Africa from the Middle East. To reach the sub-Saharan region, travelers and invaders from the north had to endure a punishing trip across the desert, moving from one isolated oasis to another. Mosquitoes and tsetse flies also killed people and their animals if they ventured to cross the desert into malarial zones.

By the nineteenth century, for West African Muslims, the quietist approach—peacefully living with animist neighbors and accepting non-Muslim elements within their own community—began to wear thin. An aggressive urge to reform and expand the community arose, particularly among intellectual elites frustrated by their memories of past glories, by the spread of literacy and knowledge of world Islamic movements, and by the social and economic upheavals brought to West Africa by the slave trade. Their dissatisfactions were similar to the complaints of today's Muslim activists. Islamist reformers rekindled a militant, revivalist tradition, not seen since the days of the Almoravids. Their task, they believed, was to struggle for an ideal society based on a greater emphasis on the Koran and Hadith (traditions of the Prophet) as guides to the way a Muslim should live and a society should be administered.

As a result, the nineteenth century is known as the jihadist period. It was exemplified by the career of Maba Diakhou Ba, who lived from 1809 to 1867 in the Senegambia. He began preaching in the region between the Saloum and Gambia Rivers, which was divided into small kingdoms governed by animist Mandinka rulers. Eventually, he met with the Muslim empire builder El Hajj Umar, who initiated him into a Sufi brotherhood and encouraged him to wage holy war against lapsed Muslims and nonbelievers. The Sufis were important to the story then and to the African Muslim community now. At this time, the pre-Islamic Senegambian states were torn by disputes between pastoralists and agriculturalists and merchants and their rulers.

After conquering the region, Maba imposed Islamic government on large areas previously untouched by Islam. He appointed Muslim judges to administer the Sharia and established schools throughout the region. However, Maba's desire to unify the whole of Senegambia ran into conflict with the recently arrived French. First they collaborated with him, later they feared his power and temporarily exiled him, and finally they killed him in battle in 1867. Another jihadist state was created in northern Nigeria by the theologian-warrior Uthman Dan Fodio, who made wholesale conversions in the northern and middle regions of modern Nigeria and eventually brought over nearly half of the Yoruba population in the South.

The jihadists failed to establish lasting states but opened the door to fundamental change, spreading Islam widely and providing the model admired by present-day reformers. A word about jihads: in nineteenth-century West Africa, jihads were wars waged against nonbelievers, but they were fought most bitterly against Muslims considered lax in their practices. Violence was and is the last and least emphasized resort for those seeking reform and change. The jihad of the word in bringing about reform and conversion to Islam usually suffices for all but the very few.

Islam first came to East Africa in the seventh century by way of ocean traders from Arabia and later from the west, across the Sahel, from the upper Niger River region. In East Africa, the rise of Islam took much longer than in West Africa to reach the peoples of the Horn and further south, down the coast. The Christian kingdom of Ethiopia, the African state nearest to the Middle East, was the stopper that kept the Muslim genie in the bottle. It was strong enough to fend off incursions from Arabia and maintain control of the African Red Sea coast. However, communities of Muslim traders, paying tribute to Ethiopian rulers, were peacefully established along major land routes to Addis and as far as Zeila in future Somaliland. Over time, these communities gave birth to a chain of small Somali states that lived off the trade in slaves, ivory, and gold with the animist states further south, which paid tribute to Ethiopia. Only in the fifteenth century, did harsher Ethiopian rule make these people think of themselves primarily as Muslims rather than as traders, and plans to launch a jihad against Ethiopia became a unifying force. But the arrival of the Portuguese was a setback, and the gold trade passed from Muslim hands and aborted Muslim expansion. Further south, from the thirteenth century on, Omani and other traders sailed down the coast, also seeking slaves. They tried to move inland but failed to find any large state system in the interior with which to trade. So they stayed in trading settlements on the coast as far south as the Zambezi River. Their presence eventually created a Swahili-speaking Muslim culture, mixing African and Arab elements in the coastal populations of Mozambique, Zanzibar, Pemba, Mombassa, and the Lamu islands. These settlements eventually became prosperous Muslim city-states in the eighteenth century.

In the nineteenth century, the spread of Islamic beliefs was dramatized politically by the appearance of the Mahdi in the Sudan, the Hanafi legal system was established as the court code, and brotherhoods became the salient organizing feature of the Sudanese Muslim community. From early on, for the Sudanese, "to be Muslim is to be Arab," and ties were strong with Egypt and the Arabian Peninsula. Further south, the Muslim communities of Ethiopia, Eritrea, and the Horn were less subjected to an influx of Arab Muslims. The gateway to these communities was the Red Sea and Indian Ocean trade, which settled Arabs and Persians on the coast from the time of the hijra on, although their presence was less frequent in the interior, except in the Sudan, Somalia, and Ethiopia. By the nineteenth century, Zanzibar was ruled by Omani Arabs, who imported the Ibadi school of law. East Africa is also the one African area where there is a strong Shia community, the result of twentieth-century Indian and Pakistani immigration.

Islam in southern Africa was introduced by political exiles brought there by the Dutch East India Company in the mid-seventeenth century. Possibly 200 such people settled near Cape Town between 1652 and 1795, when the company's possessions passed into British hands. Among their numbers was a prominent figure, Shaykh Yusuf, an Islamic saint and political activist from Indonesia. Next came approximately 3,000 convict workers, forced laborers from the Indian subcontinent ordered to work on the expanding settlement and harbors. Many Muslims were among their numbers, including several imams, whom the Dutch called Mahometaanse priesters. To these numbers were added 63,000 slaves, mostly transported from the Indian Ocean since the Dutch estates forbade the company from taking slaves on the West Coast of Africa. The company did not allow its slaves and indentured servants to practice their religion in public; thus clandestine manifestations of religion became an early feature of South African Islam, which from the start was a minority religion. People met privately in homes to pray, often gathering at the tombs of Sufi saints as well.

The first mosque was built in Cape Town in 1698, and gradually a small but educated class of Cape Muslims emerged, merchants and professional people, gravitating around individual imams and mosques. As teachers and pastors, these religious leaders founded individual congregations, and their energies were inwardly directed toward their people. Cooperation among mosques was rare, and interactions were at a local level. Thus when an imam tried to pass on his position to a son, brother, or nephew at retirement, there was often widespread resistance, and numerous succession disputes made their way into civil courts.

South Africa's favorable maritime location made passage to Egypt and the Arabian Peninsula possible by the early nineteenth century, and the number of South Africans making the hajj was large. Conversely, there were also accounts of Islamic scholars from the Middle East who were visiting South Africa. The small South African Muslim community was highly literate; many of its members were clerks or professional people, numerous mosques and schools were established, and manuscripts were circulated in an Arabic-Afrikaans script.

The Islamic presence in South Africa changed after the British abolition of slavery in 1838. Indians were imported in large numbers to work in mines and sugarcane fields, work the local African peoples disdained, and between 1860 and 1911 some 176,000 Indians were brought to Natal. Their numbers included Muslims, and others arrived as passenger Indians, as fare-paying merchants were called. A characteristic of Islam in Natal was governance by strong mosque committees rather than by individual imams. By the early twentieth century, the third regional Islamic configuration was added in the Transvaal, the result of internal migrations.

During the late twentieth century, three tendencies appeared in the South African Islamic community. First, there was a split between traditionalists and modernists similar to differences evident elsewhere in Africa. Should Islamic beliefs remain as they were in the time of the Prophet, or could they be subject to modern interpretations, fitting changing times? Second, the South African Islamic community, despite its small numbers (504,000 members in 1996),[14] produced some heroic and creative figures. Imam Abdullah Haron, a progressive imam, youth worker, and well-known preacher, was killed by the South African police in 1969. He became a martyr alongside Steve Biko. The Claremont Road Mosque invited a woman to preach, and women assumed a more equal status in that congregation than in others in Africa, worshiping on the main floor of the mosque and having their counsel actively sought in the body's deliberations. Third, as South African society faced disintegrative tensions, the same stresses were mirrored in the country's Islamic community. Extremist groups, like the People Against Grangsterism and Drugs, have committed summary executions and have taken the law into their own hands, but the South African Islamic community in general remains a conservative one.

Since Independence: A Growing Global Awareness

The most dramatic growth of the African Islamic community has taken place since independence, with an increasing participation in the world

Islamic movement, particularly since the Khomeini revolution in Iran. For a while, after 1979, African Muslims thought the promised land was just around the corner and rushed to support it. But some of the luster wore thin as they encountered the racial and religious snobbery of Iranian and North African Muslims. Memories of Arab slaveholding and mistreatment and rumors of slaveholding today in Sudan and Mauritania have convinced many Africans that ethnic, cultural, and political divisions established historically still hold true even within a community of believers.

The Iranian revolution provides a model of political activism for Muslims in sub-Saharan Africa. Iranian influence there continues to be significant despite the loss of Khomeini, its charismatic leader. Part of Iran's appeal for African Muslims comes from not being part of Arab Islam. Iranian officials have assiduously wooed the African Muslim community with frequent clerical delegations and visits by the foreign minister and Iranian president.

In East Africa, influential Muslim political activists, such as Saidi Musa, publish a political-religious message heavily inspired by the Iranian example. Highly visible student groups, such as the Muslim Students Society in Nigeria, promote the Iranian revolutionary model and have become focal points of pro-Iranian activity. As far away as South Africa, Muslims belonging to the militant Qiblah organization follow the Iranian Islamist political line. African Islamists energetically deny the relevance of doctrinal differences between the Shia—"followers of Ali," to which Iranians belong—and the Sunni, which include nearly all of the African Muslim community, dismissing attention to these differences as a Western attempt to divide the Muslim community. However, Tehran's failure to introduce social reforms and the loss of Khomeini's charismatic leadership have lessened the attractiveness of the Iranian model over time.

Despite the attractions of globalism, state boundaries, ethnicity, class, and language fundamentally divide the African Islamic community. It is also divided into often mutually incompatible ideological groupings that parallel the divisions in other monotheistic religions. These groups differ fundamentally in their responses to modern political, economic, and social developments. In Africa, they can be identified as secularists, modernists-progressives, conservative-traditionalists, and Islamists-fundamentalists.

For the *secularists*, religion is a matter of private conscience, not politics. Adherents are few in number but frequently hold high offices in African states. Their influence is relatively limited and waning. For example, Nigeria's finance minister during the recent transition period was Ismaila Usman. A Harvard graduate, he was once deputy governor of the

Central Bank of Nigeria until he questioned a payment to the corrupt, brutal President Abacha. His is a personal rather than political Muslim position, and his counterparts can be found in central banks, businesses, and ministerial offices throughout Africa.

The *modernists-progressives* represent a new development in Islam. They look analytically at Islamic tenets and believe one must not apply Islamic laws too literally or try to transpose seventh-century systems into a twenty-first-century setting. Looking behind the Koranic text to reformulate the principle, they call this process *itjihad* or individual interpretation, and find no contradiction between Islam and modernity. Such persons are generally neither xenophobic nor defensive toward westerners. Some Nigerian and Senegalese politicians fill this profile. The South African imam and author Moulana Farid Esack is a voice for such a tendency, as are some of the Muslim intellectuals who gather around the Claremont Main Road mosque.

Conservatives-traditionalists make up the largest group of African Muslims today. Belonging to the Sufi brotherhoods for the most part, they follow the prescriptions of a religious establishment with a historically frozen point of view, and they have considerable effect on politics and gender issues. This is the formula most village imams follow. Emphasizing the traditions of their forefathers and a mystical belief in the experience of a firsthand relationship with God, they also observe many pre-Islamic superstitions, such as female genital mutilation, which is prevalent in many areas of East and West Africa. These traditionalists say that female circumcision is a religiously approved custom. But that actually is not true—it has purely pre-Islamic pagan origins. Many of these traditionalist clerics have been incorporated into an informal bureaucracy by central governments. In Nigeria, for example, military regimes have turned the northern emirs into servants of the state, funding them and calling on them to keep order. This close association and employment for often unpopular secular ends has in some cases weakened Islamic institutions, tarnishing their religious credentials and making them responsible for the misdeeds of their political sponsors. In Senegal, the brotherhoods are closely allied with the ruling political system, which uses them as intermediaries between the government and the population. Young Mourides, employing state-of-the-art telecommunications and computer technology, are teaching the older faithful new, reformed Islam through audiotapes and videotapes. Through such means they hope to change Senegal's cozy brotherhood-government political and economic systems to something more Islamic and less Western oriented.

All of this has contributed to a dramatic increase in the size of a fourth

ideological grouping, the *Islamists-fundamentalists*—again part of the cy-
clical process of conservatism and reform.

The Islamist Challenge

Islamist groups are still a small minority in Africa's Muslim population,
but their call for renewal and social justice over time is likely to appeal
to many young Muslims, particularly if the economies of African states
fail to improve. For its adherents, Islamism has become "the ideology of
the dispossessed."[15]

The Wahabi movements, founded in Arabia in the eighteenth century,
and the Iranian revolutionary model have been instrumental in encouraging attacks on saint worship and other Sufi "innovations" by numbers
of reformist organizations in Africa. Although feared by moderate Muslims
in Senegal, Mali, and Nigeria, this wave of reform is nourished by pilgrims'
contacts on the hajj and by dissemination of theological materials from
the Middle East. It is supported by the middle generation of Islamists in
Mali, where it has appealed to the prosperous business class, and in Nigeria, where Abubakar Gumi, a charismatic northern Muslim leader
closely tied to Saudi Arabia, built a national political-religious following
for a reform program. In the 1970s he was one of the sole elements holding together the Nigerian Muslim community by means of his preaching,
his nationwide radio program, and his strongly expressed antichurch political positions. For a while in the early 1990s, it seemed that Gumi would
knit Nigerian Islamists into a unified political force, but his death in 1992
has left the group, for the present at least, rudderless and without national
leadership.

The shift of population to the cities also favors Islamist groups, providing access to large numbers of people cut off from their traditional
religious roots. In Tanzania, for example, the government-directed policy
of grouping people into village units is contributing to the rise of Islamist,
as well as Christian fundamentalist, groups. The focus of Islamist groups
is as heavily political as it is theological. In Nigeria, for example, groups
such as the 'Yan Izala and radical student organizations will continue to
contribute to the politicization of Islam. As one Islamist leader put it in
urging men to allow their wives to register for federal elections, "Politics
are more important than prayer."[16]

The Muslim Brotherhood, led by Ibrahim Zak Zaky and based in the
northern Nigerian city of Kano, emerged as the only independent political

voice in the North as Nigeria's military leadership looted the country's treasury and ruthlessly dealt with real and imagined enemies. The brotherhood calls for a return from Sufi syncretic mysticism to stark doctrinal basics and an end to government corruption, and it is likely to directly challenge both religious and secular establishments in coming years because of its ability to field thousands of followers to demonstrate in city streets throughout the North.

Notwithstanding, the Islamists will find it difficult to overcome ethnic and linguistic differences among Muslim populations even within single states. In Nigeria, for example, the Muslim community can not erase the long-established divisions between the Hausa and Fulani North and the Yoruba South.

Issues the African Islamist revival addresses include the following:

- Constitutional reform, with a return to preeminence of the Sharia, rather than modernized civil and criminal law codes for the judicial system
- A model for a more cosmopolitan and modern social and economic order that institutionalizes an equitable distribution of the fruits of labor and anticorruption measures
- Reform of political leadership, with a "just ruler" serving the population rather than himself
- Condemnation of lax morals, the breakdown of family unity, deviation from the dietary and drinking rules of Islam, and the mingling of sexes in school and commerce
- Incorporation of modern technology and education into the institutions of the Islamic community while denouncing Western influences
- Direct or indirect support of terrorist groups, such as in the Kenya and Tanzania American embassy bombings. Most likely the African groups will be used for logistical support in such operations, but embittered groups, such as PAGAD and Qiblah in South Africa, could institute terrorist activities locally in line with their own capabilities.

The growing Islamist presence is critical of existing religious establishments and in sermons and publications will demand social justice, equality, and international solidarity with other Islamist groups and governments historically linked to them and favorable to their cause, such as Iran, Iraq, Saudi Arabia, and Libya. Although the creation of Islamic societies and states within the boundaries of existing nations is a primary

Islamist goal, there is also a vision of a global religious and political unity that would gather all into a single international entity. For such persons, the dar-es-Islam, the realm of Islam, is a lodestone.

The Islamists' chief adversaries will continue to be central governments and traditional rulers and Sufi clerics who serve as adjuncts to government authorities. Islamist elements in the Muslim community will face hostility from secular regimes that fear the political challenge presented by religious activism and the violence associated with Muslim-Christian rivalries; secular regimes will attempt to coopt or repress Islamist groups by the following methods:

- Building and controlling mosques and Islamic educational institutions and by making clerics into civil servants
- Disbanding student organizations and banning radical literature
- Trying, jailing, and even executing Islamist opposition figures
- Targeting reformist groups for security surveillance and infiltration
- Publicly equating Islamism with fanaticism and antigovernment activity

In countries where Muslims are a majority but where there are significant non-Muslim populations, a strong Islamist presence will be particularly divisive. In both Nigeria and Sudan, efforts to create an Islamic national identity will continue to cause tension and conflict. Despite the efforts of some Muslim writers to devise a model of a pluralistic Islamic state, the history of such efforts in Africa indicates that the reality will be difficult to attain. African Islam is likely to follow the process Von Sievers described in North Africa: "The ultimate problem for Islamists is that despite of the huge demographic burgeoning in all northen African countries, they have failed so far to attract more, than, at most, 20 percent of the populations. Particularly in Egypt, the broad orthodoxy of mysticism and popular Islam . . . is alive and well."[17]

Replacing generations of religious and secular leaders in control since the 1960s and 1970s, who often lack clearly designated successors, will alter the politics of religion within Africa's secular states in the next decade. The ranks of older Muslim leaders are thinning as leading clerics in the Sufi orders enter their 80s; many have already died. In Nigeria, for example, there has been a leadership vacuum at the top in the northern Muslim community since the 'Yan Izala movement became fragmented after the death of Abubakar Gumi; the Abacha government replaced a strong sultan of Sokoto, the titular head of the Nigerian Muslim community, with an elderly, less dynamic traditionalist; and the Sufi brotherhoods were left without their principal leader, who had recently died.

The Sufi brotherhoods and Islamist movements have yet to fill this vacuum or satisfy the ambitions of a maturing, younger generation hoping to lead the Nigerian Muslim community.

Muslim youths in Africa, facing unemployment and lost educational opportunities, are likely to challenge religious and secular leadership for a share of power and economic benefits. The historical precedents—frequently cited by young militants today—are the nineteenth-century jihadists who changed the political face of West Africa, led by young leaders who attacked their elders and political leaders for theological impurity and corruption. Osama bin Laden has come to be another attraction, through his skilled manipulation of the media and through his violent challenge to what he regards as American militarism and materialism, supposedly in the name of Islam. Conspicuously absent from bin Laden and other Islamists was any political program beyond a nostalgic appeal to a golden past that never was.

In Nigeria, the Muslim Brotherhood is attacking traditional emirate authorities in frequent demonstrations in northern cities and disruptive sorties into traditionalist mosques. In Senegal, where over 94% of the population is Muslim and Sufi brotherhoods have worked closely with the government to exploit the economy and maintain domestic peace, elderly clerics are likely to face similar challenges. Already, the Mouridiya leadership is concerned about future prospects for controling young migrants from the countryside, prowling the streets of Dakar without work or stabilizing social ties.

Western political and economic interests are unlikely to face a united Islamist presence in Africa. Divisions within the community will tend to neutralize political extremism and place the more sweeping aspects of the Islamist agenda, including Islamic statehood, on hold for the time being.

Although Islam can provide a bridge between competing ethnic groups and offer advantages in forming unified states in Africa, this is unlikely to be the case. Islam has proved unable to produce unity in countries strongly divided by kinship and warlord ambitions. Except to some extent in Mali and Senegal, Islam has proved unable to aid in national integration. Although Sufi brotherhoods have developed strong commercial and theological ties across state borders, they resist opportunities to cooperate with other religious groups—and other Muslims—in nation building within a state. Somalia is an extreme example. Somali nationalism has the advantage of linguistic, social, and cultural uniformity—of which Islam is a vital component—yet is unable to overcome rivalries between kinship groups.

The greatest threat to Western interests during the coming decade is not likely to come from an overwhelming wave of Muslim revolutionary change, despite the impact of September 11, 2001, events. Rather, Western interests will be challenged by internal instability generated by Muslim minorities who are denied a political voice or an acceptable standard of living. This will pose problems for states friendly to the West that are ruled by autocratic, corrupt governments or that are at an incomplete stage of democratization. Where religious divisions are emphasized by geographic and ethnic contrasts, the danger increases; it will be part of a combustible mix of causes that could threaten African states important to U.S. interests such as Nigeria and Kenya.

As Muslim communities control and proselytize traditional animist populations, resentment of Muslim political power and growing numbers will fuel tensions in such religious communities and challenge two of Africa's democracies. The 15-year fighting in the Casamance region, where Diola traditionalists and Christians resist perceived domination and settlement by people from the Islamic North, will continue to drain Senegalese resources for the immediate future and spill over to complicate Senegal's relations with neighboring Guinea-Bissau. In Nigeria, animist tribes and Christian communities in the southwestern delta, the source of much of the country's oil wealth, are in open rebellion against exploitation of their wealth by northern Muslim politicians, as well as Western oil companies.

For Sudan, with its potential for political and economic leadership in the region, prospects for resolving issues of national unity and Islam will depend on the direction new generations of leaders take in modifying the present Islamist approach to national politics. To a significant extent this will depend on the strength of the Sudanese economy, but there are no simple solutions in sight for the crisis of state and society in Sudan.

Dangers and Opportunities

Encouraged by the present political climate to settle disputes by violence, these divisions within the African Islamic community can threaten governments that are trying to establish democratic market economies. Quarrels among Muslims threaten civil order, particularly in states important to the West such as Kenya and Nigeria. In Nigeria alone, over 5,000 people are thought to have died in religious conflicts during the past 20 years, with no end in sight. South Africa's urban crime, whose victims are the middle classes, is taking tens of thousands of lives. The 400,000 middle-class Muslim Coloured and Indian population is engaged in an increasingly politicized struggle to protect itself in ways that threaten to disrupt Cape Town and the surrounding Western Cape Province. Some Muslims have formed militias under the rubric People against Gangsterism and Drugs (PAGAD), a vigilante group.

Finally, Somalia has shown that a religious belief shared by the entire population and backed up by the same language, ethnicity, and social structure is not enough to prevent other aspects of self-identity, such as clan membership or the presence of strong, feuding leaders, from driving an African society into chaos.

The result of these struggles and growth in the midst of Africa's generally deplorable social and economic conditions demonstrates that Muslim communities, despite their surging rise in membership, have largely neutralized their political impact. In Nigeria, the Muslim North has had to accept, at least for now, a Baptist southerner as president. Muslim communities in Kenya and Tanzania are on the defensive, only occasionally able to half-heartedly threaten secession in the face of overwhelming neglect by their central governments.

Expanding communications with the rest of the Muslim world will mean that new waves of reform in other areas will directly affect African Muslims. Political upheavals elsewhere that bring Islamist leadership to power will encourage such groups south of the Sahara to press for Muslim law (Sharia) and an Islamic form of government. Muslim leaders outside Africa, seeking political support in international organizations, will encourage these ties. High-level visits between Libya, Iran, and Sudan and African leaders throughout the continent, from Senegal to South Africa, will continue to provide a measure of support to African governments and Muslim communities.

Thus, Western political and economic interests are unlikely to face a united Muslim presence in Africa. Divisions within the community will neutralize political extremism and check the establishment of Islamic states south of the Sahara. The appeal of secular westernization for African societies will remain one of the greatest challenges facing militant Islamism. Localized disturbances and criminal activity by dissatisfied Muslim minorities is more likely to emerge than a dramatic Iranian-type revolution. However, grassroots violence could threaten national unity and civil order in potential regional leaders, such as Nigeria and Kenya, both countries friendly to the West. Support for terrorist groups will be provided according to the means available to local African Islamist groups. At the same time, African police and security forces will increase their surveillance of such groups, possibly leading to measures to disband or disrupt their activities.

Although Muslim communities will grow rapidly in Africa, internal factionalism is likely to continue to divide and weaken their political influence. Whether a younger generation of Islamist leadership can overcome these divisions remains to be seen. In the short term, the search for nonsecular, even utopian solutions will be curbed by the lack of resources for large-scale religious organization at the grassroots level and by the power of states' security forces.

However, the violence associated with intra-Muslim rivalries and competition with Christian populations is likely to continue, and this could threaten civil order in states with ambitions for regional leadership, as well as distract governments friendly to the West that are seeking to make their way toward a fuller democracy. On balance, a barrier to improved Western-Muslim relations in Africa is less the actual threat of Islam than Western perceptions of it, which fail to accept African Islam as part of a global movement with distinct local manifestations as diverse as the regions and peoples from which they emerge. The opportunities for westerners to make common cause with Islamic communities in Africa are multiple; most are moderate in outlook, wanting primarily a better, fuller life for members. Such communities and the countries in which they are situated have numerous unrealized possibilities for constructive religious, political, and economic interactions with the West.

Islam in Nigeria

Seeking a Competitive Edge

A Question of Conscience—Or Is It a Conspiracy?

On March 22, 2000, state officials in Zamfara—one of Nigeria's states in the far north—amputated the right hand of Mallam Buba Bello Karegarke Jangeli, a Fulani cattle dealer who had been convicted in an area court for stealing a neighbor's cows, valued at about $100. This set off a social and political crisis of national proportions, caused violent conflicts throughout the country among Nigeria's competitive religious communities, and challenged the stability of Nigeria's newly democratic government.

Two months earlier, Ahmed Sani Yerima, Zamfara's elected governor, had signed a carefully drafted law establishing a Sharia penal code for the state that prohibited prostitution, gambling, and the sale, purchase, and consumption of alcohol (A Law to Establish a Sharia Penal Code for Zamfara State, Law No. 10, 2000; January 27, 2000). As a Muslim, his conscience now was clear, the governor told those who questioned his action in Nigeria and internationally.

Soon afterward, Zamfara authorities shut down movie houses and closed bars and liquor stores. A man drinking alcohol in public was sentenced to 80 lashes with a cane in Zamfara's capital city,[1] an unemployed farm worker was offered the option of paying the equivalent of $1,580 for knocking out his wife's teeth during a quarrel or allowing her to knock out an equal number of his teeth, and a young man was given 100 lashes for having sex with an unmarried woman.[2]

In February, a local vigilante group empowered by the governor to seek out infringements of Sharia brought in Jangeli for stealing the cow. Jangeli, known locally for several years as "Karegarke" or "Ranch Raider," confessed to the crime and was sentenced by the Alkali of the area court after he pleaded guilty. Jangeli waived an appeal because he would have faced the opprobrium of the local community if he had gone free, according to one observer.

Although the amputation was rumored to have taken place in a city square before an approving crowd of several hundred—after which the wound was cauterized in boiling peanut oil—in fact, a doctor at a local hospital performed the operation, following which Jangeli was taken to the governor's house, where he remained for some time.[3] His picture, with the severed hand dangling from a rope next to him, was front-page news throughout the Nigerian press. To all inquiries, Jangeli maintained that he did not regret the sentence, which, he said, would force him to return to a properly Muslim way of life and brought him nationwide notoriety, as well as a $500 subsidy from the governor toward launching his future.

The amputation loosed a storm of criticism from southern Christians and from the majority of Nigeria's raucous press, in which the sentence was referred to as a return to barbarism and a deathblow to foreign investment in the economy. The president of the Nigerian Civil Liberties Organization, Ayo Obe, a well-known Nigerian woman lawyer, argued that stealing should not be punished by cutting off hands and decried the injustice of punishing a cow thief while those who steal billions of *naira* from the state go free.[4] For these critics and the majority of Nigeria's sometimes speculative press, the Sharia's renewed appearance was politically motivated, reflecting the governor's personal ambition and the efforts of northern Islamic leaders to reassert themselves as a political force.

Conspiracy theories ran rampant in the corridors of government buildings in Abuja, the federal capital, still under construction, as is the post-military, democratic state. Southern politicians in the Christian-led government claimed that northern power brokers, particularly among the northern military who had ruled Nigeria for most of the postindependence period, were behind the Sharia controversy in an attempt to sabotage the recently installed Olesegun Obasanjo regime. It was said that the president's slowly evolving anticorruption policies directly threatened the country's former leaders. Nobel laureate Wole Soyinka called the amputation a blow against the nation and the introduction of Sharia in the North as an act of secession.[5]

On the other hand, many northern Muslim observers—even those not particularly drawn to Governor Sani's dramatic embrace of *hudud* punishments (Mandetory Criminal Sanctions)—saw this as a genuine grassroots movement that had leapfrogged over the political elite and traditional Muslim leadership to the top of the North's political agenda. It was driven in large part by public frustration with the extremes of northern military rulers in looting the economy, leaving it in shambles. The northern population's discontent with its own leadership had produced a ground swell of support for Obasanjo's candidacy for president in 1999. Now it had created a populist backlash that turned Governor Sani—whatever his methods and goals—into "the man of the hour" in Nigeria's impoverished North.[6]

By April, neighboring northern states, including Kano, Bauchi, Niger, and Kaduna, made plans to pass similar laws. The National Council of Muslim Youth Organizations initiated a bill to introduce Sharia to Oyo State in the Southwest, where there is a substantial Muslim Yoruba community and where Muslims burned down churches in response to police attempts to control and eventually expel a controversial Muslim preacher.[7] As Muslims hailed the reintroduction of the Sharia penal code in the North as a reaffirmation of their true "Way," which had been denied them since colonial times, other segments of the population continued to express fears that they would not fare well in an Islamicized political system.[8]

The geographic dimensions of what is now Nigeria were cobbled together from the lands of the 350 to 400 or more linguistically defined ethnic groups that hugged the shores of the Niger River and Lake Chad in West Africa during the nineteenth- and twentieth-century scramble of European countries to expand their power and trade by declaring control over the region. Britain proclaimed its sovereignty over the colony in 1900 and governed the country until 1960, when Nigeria became an independent state in the form of a federation of northern, eastern, and western regions. Since then Nigeria has been further divided administratively into 36 states and the Federal Capital Territory of Abuja. Its population continues to speak in a cacophony of tongues, with three lingua franca dominating the three regions—Hausa in the North, Igbo in the East, and Yoruba in the West. The official language continues to be English.

Although the state of Nigeria came into being relatively recently, Islam had penetrated the region by means of trans-Saharan trade routes, which included the route to Wangarawa to the west and the Tripoli-Kano trans-Saharan route dating back to around the ninth century. Strong local kings were noted in the region, and in the fourteenth century Ibn Battuta described a king of Bornu who "does not appear to the people and does not address them except behind a curtain."[9] By 1500, the Hausa emirs and urban traders become at least nominally Muslim. For Hausa merchants, Islam offered many benefits: contacts with the larger Muslim world, access to credit and finance, and opportunities to marry women in other cities.[10]

It was Uthman Dan Fodio who established the Sokoto caliphate in the early nineteenth century, which covers most of what is now the North of Nigeria and to a large extent shaped the Muslim community and its present-day aspirations. It remains the reference point for many contemporary reformers, its achievements magnified in the telling.

By the end of the eighteenth century, Islamic practice had been corrupted by syncretic pagan influences introduced by Muslim teachers and the oppressive leadership of the kingdoms by Hausa rulers. Islam was progressively excluded from the political, social, and economic spheres. The splendor of purified Islamic practice was reduced to a series of "dry rituals."[11] For most of the population, instruction in the fundamental practice of Islam was virtually nonexistent. Though some were nominal Muslims, others had not even "smelt the smell of Islam."[12]

At the time of the jihad, Hausaland was divided into two groups of states—the Hausa Bakwai (the seven original Hausa states: Kano, Zazzau, Gobir, Katsina, Daura, Rano, and Biram) and the Banza Bakwai (the seven nonrecognized states: Kabi, Zamfara, Nupe, Yawuri, Yoruba, Borgu, and Gurma).[13] Zamfara was at the height of its power in the early eighteenth century until it was annexed by Gobir. These petty kingdoms were frequently at war with each other, and by the beginning of the nineteenth century, except for Gobir, they had quarreled themselves into a decline.[14]

Similarities between the corrupt and mismanaged Hausa states against which Uthman Dan Fodio rebelled and the successive governments of the Nigerian Federation since independence are frequently cited. The Hausa kings taxed heavily and appropriated women's possessions, and ruling-class men were free to abduct women, whom they kept as concubines. Rulers were the final arbiters of law, and no one could challenge their judgments. Judges who applied the royal laws were said to be thoroughly corrupt, and plaintiffs had to bribe them for their cases to be considered at all. Corrupt judges set aside the Muslim punishments prescribed by the Sharia, commuting those for adultery, theft, and murder to fines. The fine for murder in particular was turned over to the ruler.[15]

Into this setting came Uthman Dan Fodio, a member of the Fulani linguistic-ethnic group and an inspired preacher and teacher. In 1774 he began to travel throughout Hausaland, speaking to growing crowds in local dialects of Hausa and Fulfulde, often in verse, which could be more easily memorized by largely illiterate audiences. Some of his tours lasted as long as 5 years. His aim was to purify Hausa society of un-Islamic practices and to teach the "Way" laid down by Allah through the Sharia. Uthman Dan Fodio's early successes were with ordinary people, not with the higher class Muslim scholars and Hausa kings, both of whom were threatened by his grassroots appeal and wanted to continue the status quo by putting an end to his preaching. Violent attacks culminated in the king of Gobir's ban of conversion to Islam, curbing the activities of Uthman [obscured] orbidding the wearing of Islamic dress. [obscured]

Fin[obscured] were expelled from Gobir. Their depart[obscured] ophet to escape persecution and to gat[obscured] ommunity. Uthman Dan Fodio becam[obscured] e faithful (Amir al-Mu'minin) of the Isl[obscured] ok an oath of allegiance to him, and h[obscured] ving the Muslim "Constitution," that is[obscured] the community set up a parallel state i[obscured] ir kingship, the community defeated [obscured] t few years set about conquering the no[obscured] leadership of flag bearers appointed by Uthman Dan Fodio.

The Islamic leader was the head of an extraordinary family. His brother, Abdullahi, was an important jurist who established parameters for the administration of law in the caliphate. Shehu's son, Mohammad Bello, was a scholar-jurist who defined the ideal of criminal and political justice and later administered the caliphate.[17] All three men wrote books that are considered fundamental to present-day Islamic scholarship in Nigeria. Bello's ambition was to create a just and fair political system in Hausaland. He set up the administrative institutions that were to bring this about, "based on the essential elements of the jihad ideology," which were the renewal (tajdid) of Islam and the reestablishment of justice through government based on the Sharia. Thus he emphasized leadership qualities such as "integrity, kindness, humility, abstinence, sacrifice and piety."[18] The explorer Clapperton wrote that the Koranic law was so strictly in force in Bello's time "that the whole country when not in a state of war, was so well-regulated that it is a common saying that a woman might travel with a casket of gold upon her head from one end of the Fellata dominions to the other."[19]

Although the Fulani jihadists differentiated themselves religiously, culturally, and linguistically from the Hausa majority in the Hausa kingdoms and from the Kanuri population of Borgu, their concepts of authority and power were strikingly similar by the end of the nineteenth century. The ruler (sarki) was at the apex of a centrally organized, hierarchical administrative structure within a "legitimate institutional framework."[20] He exercised absolute, God-given power over those living in the territory associated with his capital city. This included power over life and death.

These kingdoms had a long-established corporate identity. The Hausa word umma has origins that suggest links with matrilineal organization. An individual's umma may be identified in terms of birthplace; clan or family; language; country; region, district, or city ward; religion; or race.[21] Depending on circumstances, an individual may claim a primary identity defined in any of these dimensions. Attending an international gathering or participating in politics at the national level, he may identify himself primarily as Nigerian. If quarreling with neighboring groups over land rights, he may claim his kinship identity as a primary reference. In communal altercations, his religious identity becomes all-important.

Religious communities in the Sokoto empire included Muslims, people of the book (Jews and Christians), and animists. Within the Islamic community, umma described religious groups at many levels. In different situations the term referred to a group assembled for weekly prayers or the Muslim segment of a city or state population. Today, it also refers to the worldwide community of all Muslims.

In consolidating the conquered territories as the Sokoto Caliphate and its structures of authority, the first generation of Fulani "flag bearers" established a confederation of some 40 emirates that owed fealty to the sultan of Sokoto. In what are now the North and Middle Belt states (middle between North and South) of contemporary Nigeria, only the Kanuri kingdom of Borgu, with its own history of Muslim law in the Northeast, successfully resisted the jihad. Large numbers of Yoruba were also converted to Islam by Uthman Dan Fodio's followers. Throughout the caliphate only Sharia law was applied, and only the kadi courts adjudicated civil and criminal law; only traditional land law survived from an earlier era.[22]

The Sharia, which has surfaced as the principal causus belli in the latest round of Muslim-Christian conflict, was being revived, and its roots in Nigeria were traced to the confederation created by Uthman Dan Fodio's jihad. The Sharia is inseparable from Islam, advocates and detractors alike argued. As delineated by Abdullahi, Uthman Dan Fodio's brother, for the Muslim community, the leader (caliph) is required to set the parameters of justice for the community and appoint officers to administer the law, including the judge (qadi), the Vizier (wazir) and the emir (amir or governor).[23] The requirements for serving as judges in the Sokoto Caliphate include being Muslim, male, learned, adult, sane, free, and of honorable character and probity. The candidate must not be deaf or dumb. He must be paid sufficiently to protect him from the temptations of corruption, must restrict his social interaction to the minimum, must not accept gifts except from close family members, and "must avoid all but the most essential ceremonies—all to reduce the temptation for corruption."[24] Such restrictions were to prevent the use of office for private gain rather than religious service. The legal system included qadis with general responsibilities and specialists, such as those dealing only with marriage issues (women's qadis) or with supervision of orphans' properties.

Uthman Dan Fodio's brother, Shehu Abdullahi, was charged with constructing the system of justice for the Sokoto Caliphate. He broadened its scope by putting his followers under no obligation to adopt one specific school of law. The law was to be based on the Sharia as laid down in the Koran, Sunnah, and *ijma* (consensus) of the Muslim community. When no clear provisions for a case have been laid down, the judge may resort to *ijtihad*, or judgments by legal scholars.[25]

The power of emirate leadership in the North was frozen in place during the colonial era. Gradually the role of Sharia was whittled down, until, in the 1960s, it was limited to Islamic personal law. Frederick Lugard, the first high commissioner of northern Nigeria, developed the British system of indirect rule, allowing governmental institutions already existing there to continue to function under a colonial superstructure. Thus, Britain ruled through the Muslim caliphate rulers, perpetuating the leadership of Sokoto and Borno. The British encouraged northern rulers to distance themselves from Western culture—unlike the assimilationist peoples of the Southeast and West.

But the British arrival in northern Nigeria brought a different and contrasting legal system. Indirect rule introduced British law, in addition to the native law established by the Native Court Proclamation of 1900, which was largely drawn from the Sharia. Each legal system had its own courts. Although ordinarily a Muslim was automatically subject to Islamic law, in Nigeria under the British and since independence a Muslim could opt for either system.[26] In the North, most native courts were the emir or Alkali courts, and the law administered for the most part was Sharia law of the Maliki school. In return for cooperation in ruling the North, the British allowed the Muslim emirates wide latitude in maintaining the conservative orthodoxy of the Fulani jihad. It had been preserved virtually intact, and as a result, as late as 1960, the Sharia was "more widely, and in some respects more rigidly, applied in Northern Nigeria than anywhere outside Arabia."[27] In addition to private, family, or Muslem personal law, native law covered criminal law, even capital cases. In fact it is estimated that over 90% of criminal cases in the North were tried in native courts.[28] In criminal cases the native courts could award any punishment "subject to the condition that no inhuman treatment could be inflicted. And they could not inflict the penalty of death." Nor had they jurisdiction on "non-native individuals or local inhabitants who were in government service."[29]

The first Muslim Court of Appeal, to which all civil and criminal cases decided in native courts (later replaced by the Sharia Court of Appeal) under Islamic law were to be referred, was created by the British colonial administration in 1956. By 1960, however, its jurisdiction was limited to Islamic personal law, which included marriage, trusteeship, and inheritance. After 1960, although criminal law from the Sharia was supplanted by British law, the Alkali courts continued to have jurisdiction in both civil cases and criminal cases, provided they applied British common law in the latter.[30]

Recent years have witnessed something of a role reversal in the role of Islam in Nigeria, a switch from being the religion of a segment of society determined to preserve its status to one advocating fundamental societal change. Ameer Ali points out that Islamism as a movement for freedom and independence is a relatively recent phenomenon.[31] The history of military and civilian governments for the most part under northern Muslim leadership brought little benefit to the northern populations. The grip of the largely Muslim and conservative leadership of the North persisted after independence and only began to loosen with the development of democratic institutions at the local government level. As the geographic regions were broken up into states, Muslim control diminished and in some cases was eliminated when Muslim numbers were not large.[32]

The present representational issues have proved a barrier to effectively counting the population as powerful communities compete for national assets. In contemporary Nigeria, the Muslim community is unevenly distributed, with 73% in the North and Middle Belt regions, and is divided between the Northwestern (more than 90%) and some of the central states, with as little as 10% Muslim membership in Benue State. There is also a sizable Muslim population in Yorubaland in the South.[33]

Muslim populations in the eastern region appeared in the wake of Muslim traders who settled in Elele before 1896. Despite the Civil War of 1967–1970, when the East withdrew from the federation and the Muslim population fell precipitously, the number of mosques in the region has grown to 65 in the Niger Delta, with growing Islamic populations in the area of Port Harcourt also.[34]

The *mallam* (Islamic scholar) in highly stratified Hausa society enjoyed a social ranking second only to the emir. Official estimates of the number of *mallams* living in northern Nigeria was 25,000, with over a quarter of a million pupils; by 1960 that figure had risen to some 50,000.[35] In his study of the history of Kano, John Paden writes that about half of the *mallams* continue to teach Islamic studies to children in Koranic schools. The rest are otherwise employed—many of them in trade, tailoring, and farming.[36] Hausa *mallams* design and sew the intricately decorated caps worn by men in northern Nigeria. *Mallams* are the beneficiaries of annual donations by the emir. *Zakat*—required Islamic alms obligatory for all Muslims with a minimal taxable income—are given once a year to *mallams* by all strata of society. They keep part of this tax and give the rest to the poor.[37]

A Divided Muslim Community

The Muslim community is divided into several separate categories. One is made up of groups that emphasize issues of identity. A second includes groups whose approach is the jihad of the word, by which they hope to reform and revitalize Nigerian Muslim society through education and training and by legal means achieve an Islamic society through the values of Sharia. A third category, often voiced among the dispossessed and of those who seek to speak for them, advocates hard-line reforms that presuppose a transformation of political and social institutions from the bottom up—a sweeping revolutionary change, after which the political and economic structures can be rebuilt within the dimensions of a strictly interpreted and universally applied Sharia. These categories change, however, as political circumstances and ranks of leaders and enemies are altered. Muslim-Christian issues—such as Sharia law and membership in the OIC—help to unify and define Nigeria's Islamic community, but it remains for the most part divided by economic, as well as cultural and religious, differences, and these divisions, which have threatened civil order in the past, could do so again.

Muslims have endured suffering from the excesses of military rule and egregious accumulation of wealth by northern military officers. As the Nigerian economy slipped to the level of a global basket case, the North and North Central regions, far removed from the coastal commercial centers of international trade and lagging in infrastructure and industrial development, were among the hardest hit. As Nigeria's wealth poured out by the billions of dollars into private accounts of senior military officers, virtually none trickled down to the poor or to a devastated middle class, struggling to survive the dual burdens of inflation and corruption. As a result, a clearly marked class differentiation has grown within the Islamic community. There is a wide gap between the rich and the poor, and a deep rift has appeared between those Muslims associated with the military regimes and Muslim educated elites.

The Muslim League for Accountability (MULAC) is attempting to address this trend by setting Muslim standards for public service based on Koranic prohibitions against corruption and promoting requirements for "Islamic" ethics in business, such as using honest weights and measures. A list of league sponsors reads like a *Who's Who* of moderate northern Muslim organizations and includes the Islamic Trust of Nigeria, the Waff Road Mosque Forum, and the Federation of Muslim Women's Associations of Nigeria, among others.

The nearly 60 million members of the Nigerian Muslim community remain divided between the establishment Sufi traditionalist majority and a vocal Islamist minority. Most Nigerian Muslims are Sunni of the Maliki school, but among them many belong to Tijaniya and Qadiriya Sufi brotherhoods, which have acquired unique characteristics during their centuries-long presence in the area.

Opposed to them are the reformists, who range in approach from moderate to extremist. Their popularity can be measured by the distribution of as many as 20 million copies of the Koran in Hausa, translated by northern reformist leader Abubakar Gumi, whose 'Yan Izala organization achieved national stature before his death in 1992. His Hausa translation is attacked by the Sufi brotherhoods (any change from the Arabic wording of the original revelation is considered by some to be heretical) in heated debates each year on television during Ramadan, the Muslim month of fasting. Gumi set the standard for Muslim reform for over 20 years, criticizing the Sufis' emphasis on saintly intermediaries and extra prayers beyond the daily five required by Islam. These differences provoked violent confrontations in the 1980s between the 'Yan Izala and Sufi traditionalists in the North. By the time of his death, Gumi had begun to draw the whole community with him toward the center. Since then, however, without Gumi's leadership, the 'Yan Izala has fragmented and new organizations are emerging at the grassroots level.

The most prominent of these at present is the Muslim Brotherhood led by Ibrahim Zak Zaky, a university lecturer with Iranian ties who went to jail during the Abacha period but was released during the 1998 transition. The press calls him Shia because he has studied in Iran and praises the Iranian political model—but Zak Zaky denies that he is Shia. Although highly critical of the Sufi brotherhoods, Zak Zaky was released at the urging of northern elites who feared that prolonged imprisonment only increased his popularity. During his time in prison, his Muslim Brotherhood grew to an estimated 10,000 members and was constantly involved in disruptive demonstrations in Zaria, Kaduna, and Kano. Zak Zaky's sometimes unorthodox teachings include authorization of temporary marriages, which enable bypassing the often exorbitant costs of the traditional bride price, and insistence that his followers go unarmed to noisy political demonstrations.

Zak Zaky's views came to prominence in the aftermath of the September 11 terrorist attacks in New York and Washington. Speaking at Days of Martyrs in Zaria, the Muslim cleric called the American attacks on Afghanistan a war on Islam and Muslims, although the government of Nigeria came out in support of the military action. It was the Israeli secret service, not Osama bin Laden, that destroyed the World Trade Center, Zak Zaky concluded, in order to bring about a greater Israel.[38]

Among the issues that divide the community is the change in the position of Muslim women. Although some mosques, including the principal mosque in Abuja, continue to seat women separately from men, the charismatic reformer Abubakar Gumi actively lobbied for an equal role and a political voice for women. He and the cluster of Islamic organizations associated with him—including the Rabita, the Islamic Foundation in Kano, and the Islamic Education Trust (IET)—have supported the Federation of Muslim Women's Associations of Nigeria (FOMWON) in the face of bitter opposition. By now, some 100 groups in the North and over 300 in the South, pushing for political mobilization and women's education, have affiliated with the organization. Although the daughters of the former sultan of Sokoto, Ibrahim Dasuki, have joined FOMWON, elite organizations hostile to change, such as the Muslim Sisters' Organization, continue to agitate for traditional veiling and modest dress codes for women. Tensions between both camps show no indications of abating.

Much of the punch has temporarily gone out of the Islamic community's leadership, and that has probably contributed to their lack of resistance to the principle of shared power. In addition to Muslim leaders who were destroyed by the Abacha government and the older postindependence generation that is dying off, a generation of their successors—between the ages of 20 and 35—has been lost to the Muslim community. Educated Nigerians from the North, as well as the South, have left the country in large numbers, driven out by rampant inflation, corruption, and oppressive military government.

Part of this leadership vacuum is being filled by northern reformist groups, such as Ibrahim Zak Zaky's Muslim Brotherhood, which draws heavily on foot soldiers recruited from among unemployed young migrants to northern cities from rural areas and neighboring countries hard hit by drought and poverty. Zak Zaky built a national reputation as the one independent northern political voice speaking up against the Abacha regime. Although he and his youthful following may seek solutions to problems of poverty and unemployment in Islamic militancy, limited resources and the strength of government security forces will tend to curb the possibilities of overwhelming demonstrations or large-scale organization at the grassroots level.

The essence of Sufism is a personal relationship with God. With training, an individual reaches higher stages of this relationship. The leaders of the Fulani jihad were products of this school of Islamic thought, and Shehu, Abdullahi, and Mohammad Bello all wrote extensively on it. In the Sufi tradition, a *shehu* teaches and acts as intercessor, conveying God's messages to the faithful. A master also associates himself with a founding saint of a brotherhood that is incorporated with initiation procedures and rituals. In northern Nigeria, the two principal brotherhoods are the Qadiriya and Tijaniya, both of which were founded in North Africa. Most of the Fulani jihad's leaders were members of the Qadiriya, and thus nineteenth-century *mallam* and ruling classes were also in the Qadiriya. Original contact with the Tijaniya came through Umar Futi, who visited the region at the beginning of the nineteenth century. It was again introduced by North African *mallams* in the early colonial period and became part of the reaction against Fulani domination of Hausa and other non-Fulani groups. The movement was again given renewed vigor when Ibrahim Niass, a Senegalese *shehu*, visited the region in 1937. Niass's landmark event was to bring Hausa and Fulani *mallams* together. His followers were referred to in Paden's study as Reformed Tijaniya, with the principal leaders in Kano being Emir Abdullahi Bayero and his successor, Muhammad Sanusi. The Qadiriya underwent a similar revival under the leadership of Nasiru Kabara. Leadership of the two brotherhoods by the mid-twentieth century had become almost entirely Nigerian, and the Tijaniya brotherhood is probably the largest Muslim group in Nigeria today.[39] Reforms undertaken from within the brotherhoods extended their membership "from an elite to a mass base" and have brought Nigerian Muslims into contact with the wider Islamic world. These "reformed" Muslims are not afraid of using all new developments in technology, have drawn together a mix of ethnic members, and are largely urban oriented.[40]

Conflict within the contemporary Islamic community during the 1950s and 1960s was primarily between the Tijaniya and Qadiriya brotherhoods. In an effort to unite the warring sects, the Sardauna established an Islamic Advisory Committee in 1963, with limited success. It was only with the emergence of the Izala movement in the 1970s that the brotherhoods, realizing the threat to their position, drew together against the common enemy.[41] A new corporate identity emerged, known as the Darika, a Hausa version of traditional Sufi Muslim brotherhoods (tariqa) found throughout West Africa.[42]

The Jama'at Izalatil Bidia Was Iqamatus Sunnah (Movement Against Negative Innovations and for Orthodoxy), known as the Izala, is primarily dedicated to reforming the Muslim community and freeing it from pre-Islamic and un-Islamic practices promoted by the dominant tariqa. The Izala has been committed to responding to the cultural changes introduced by forces from outside the community and to maintaining "the clear lines of Islamic identity."[43] Thus, although members work to convert non-believers, most of their effort is focused within the Muslim community itself. They have no particular program for replacing the secular with an Islamic state, provided the state does not interfere with their worship or preaching. Furthermore, although highly critical of the tariqas, they also have patrons at high levels of government and their (Izala) leadership is largely drawn from the civil service, which helps account for the group's relatively high educational level and urban influence.[44]

Established Muslim groups also found themselves threatened during the 1980s by an unorthodox sect, the Maitatsine, which rejected the "materialism" of orthodox Islam and emerging modern technology while ascribing divine powers and authority to the sect's leader, Mohammed Marwa Maitatsine.[45] Coming from a Mahdist tradition, Maitatsine crossed all boundaries by proclaiming himself greater than the Prophet Muhammad. His strident, militant preaching against corruption in Nigeria and the world resulted in violent clashes with security forces, and between 1980 and 1984 more than 5,000 people were killed in riots, many of them in Kano, where Maitatsine died as well.[46]

During the 1990s, the Darika also confronted the growing popularity of a "Shia" movement, the Muslim Brotherhood, which focuses on a politically activist reform movement under the charismatic leadership of the

Zaria-based Ibrahim Zak Zaky (b. 1963). Unlike the Izala, the brother-hood has no large following in the civil service.[47] (According to his interview in *Equal Justice*, Zak Zaky studied at Nigerian universities and has visited Iran a number of times. However, he claims that the movement is self-funding by its approximately 500,000 members).[48]

"We envisage a society which agrees with the message of God. We are Moslems and Islam is our system of life. So, we also envisage a nation, which should be wholly Islamic, Islamic in the sense that it considers Allah as the Lord of the nation" (statement by Ibrahim Zak Zaky, July 1996).[49]

The Muslim Brotherhood charges the traditional brotherhoods with accepting the secular nature of the Nigerian state. Zak Zaky argues that the sect is morally bankrupt through this association with corrupt secular government at every level from local to national. His political militancy has roots in the Shia doctrine of the imam as the political and religious leader of the *umma*, by which every authority is legitimized, whereas the less overtly political Sunni majority has no fundamental objection to state authorities who do not attempt to tamper with their religious practice. Although criticizing *tariqa* mysticism and alleged pre-Islamic practices, the brotherhood has not insisted on a particular format in prayer services, unlike the Izala, who prefer to attend their own mosques under their own imams.[50]

Like the Maitatsine, the Muslim Brotherhood activism has also rejected the state's authority to rule on religious matters, drawing the group into controversy with political and security forces. In the standoff between the brotherhood and civil authorities at Katsina in 1991, at issue was a planned demonstration by the brotherhood against a press report that it said slandered the Prophet. Although forbidden to demonstrate by state authorities, members marched nevertheless. The governor, seeing this as a direct challenge to his authority, called out the army and police.[51]

In 1994, brotherhood members broke into the prison in Kano and chased away the staff in order to remove a non-Muslim accused of using paper torn from a Koran as toilet paper. Members deny press reports that they then beheaded the offender and paraded the severed head through the streets of Kano.[52]

The Abacha regime tangled frequently with the brotherhood and jailed its leaders, including Zak Zaky for over 2 years (he has served 9 years in prison overall) on charges of sedition, using as evidence a magazine cover motto distributed by the brotherhood that read, "There is no government except that of Islam." Zak Zaky's followers clashed frequently with state forces during 1997 while protesting the detention of their members, hundreds of whom were imprisoned.[53] Zak Zaky's was the only voice from the North in opposition to the corrupt, brutal Abacha regime.

Despite his success in rallying followers in the cause of political and religious reform during the 1990s, Zak Zaky has assumed a low profile in the 2000 Sharia conflict. Early on he dissociated himself from the Zamfara legislative effort, saying it was premature to try to impose Sharia in a society that lacked sufficient Muslim education and political institutions. Unlike the Izala, Zak Zaky has indicated that he is uninterested in reform within the present political system, whether or not it is democratic. He maintains that loyalty to an oppressive, un-Islamic government encourages "falsehood, iniquity, and corruption."[54] This was a point he repeated after the adoption of Sharia in Zamfara State, arguing that Sharia as an Islamic legal system could only be adopted by an Islamic government and that "for now" Nigeria is a constitutional state. Moreover, Governor Ahmed Sani "has an idea of what he wants but he mistakenly called it Sharia."[55]

The Muslim Brotherhood's largest publicity makers are its processions and ceremonies, which are often broken up by the police, thus making them newsworthy to the press. The brotherhood also sponsors lectures in schools and mosques, conducts seminars, publishes magazines and books, and offers assistance in mediating disputes.

Zak Zaky's goal is nothing less than the total transformation of society from top to bottom along the lines of Iran's Muslim theocracy. Until such institutions are in place—and the economy offers the possibility to the common person of achieving an acceptable standard of living—Zak Zaky believes that it is unrealistic to demand adherence to the rigors of Islamic law. He is prepared to pursue his adversarial aims either by peaceful means of persuasion or by militant jihad. During the honeymoon period of high hopes in democracy, he is willing to stand aside, ready to reengage when the time appears to be appropriate. In the meantime, he claims that his is the only political party in the country—that the other parties "are selected by the government from the same club of thieves who ruined this country." Elsewhere, he has said that the brotherhood is not a group but a movement.[56]

Conspicuous actors in both the Maitatsine and Muslim Brotherhood movement, particularly when active measures against security forces were involved, were youthful Muslim students and the impoverished street gangs of unemployed youths. Traditionally, parents sent their children to study with *mallams* (Islamic scholars), who were paid for their services by the labor of the students in the *mallam's* fields. Students were fed by the charity of people in the community. The hardships suffered by many students in this system have been described by the Nigerian novelist Ibrahim Tahir in *The Last Imam*.[57]

The *almajiranci* system, as it is now called (historically the word referred to the people who gave up wealth and family to follow the Prophet's hijra to Medina) is a semiformal, Islamic educational system that attracts poor students, ages 4 to 16, who are unable to afford a Western education. In the past they were supported by the charity of district or village communities, but during the past 20 years, as the economy has degenerated, sources of food and shelter have dried up except among the very rich. The *almajiranci* have become one of the principal sources of street begging. Large numbers have migrated from rural areas to the cities, where they haunt markets, sports stadiums, mosques, intersections, post offices, and secretariats. Muslims, as well as Christians, criticize the custom, blaming it on social mores and disclaiming any connection of begging with Islam. In Dickensian fashion, northerners believe that begging for some has become a profession, with "executive beggars" fielding armies of children who collect for them. The problem is not only localized in Nigeria; it is estimated that over 90% of the beggars in Saudi Arabia are professionals from Nigeria who are working for "executives."[58]

These groups of young people are readily recruited for mob violence in communal disputes in Nigeria. An early example was Maitatsine Marwa's sect, which recruited at bus stops and markets. The Muslim Brotherhood, like the Izala, has also appealed to them, particularly the unemployed, who provide the brotherhood with dedicated preachers, organizers, trouble shooters, and network links;[59] also their efficient communications and transportation systems make it easy to mobilize support from bases throughout the North. The group runs fleets of buses within cities and across the region. The *almajiranci* attract crowds of sympathizers among the urban poor by their aggressiveness and their willingness to seek martyrdom.[60]

Seeking the Competitive Edge

More than most of Africa's Muslim communities, Nigeria's is focused on a competitive struggle with the nearly numerically equal Christian community. Based on the results of the latest census (1963), Nigeria's people number some 110 million, with Muslim and Christian communities running nearly even and an ever-diminishing balance of traditional animists.

For the most part, the Muslim community has lived peacefully along-side its Christian counterpart. Intermarriage is frequent, and Christian traders move frequently about Muslim lands and vice versa, followed by growing patterns of settlement in the South by many northern Muslims, who are engaged in commerce.

Muslim-Christian relations in the eastern region have been peaceful, despite active missionary work on both sides among local animist populations and occasional disputes over land ownership. However, there were some retaliatory killings of Muslims in the East by local people for a massacre of Christian southerners in Kano by soldiers (the majority of whom turned out to have been Christian).[61]

Christians frequently claim that they have been refused land rights for building churches and have difficulties obtaining time on television and radio in the North for Christian programming that would reach sizable Christian communities there. From the beginning of the Obasanjo administration, religious differences continued to simmer beneath the surface and soon posed daunting problems for the new government, problems that it generally ignored.

Muslim-Christian cooperation remains fragile. One of the issues that has been used to define Muslim identity in Nigeria has been its long-standing competition with the vigorously evangelical Christian community. For most of the past 20 years, tension and violence have characterized relations between these two communities.

Religious fault lines are still operative, particularly when seconded by ethnic and economic differences, as the recent standoff in Lagos between Hausa Muslims, wanting pasturage for their cattle, and Yoruba Christian landowners has demonstrated. Then, in May 2000, just as national reconciliation seemed to have succeeded, 100 people were killed in Kafanchan in communal rioting.

One of the issues that continues to provoke conflict is the role of Islamic law in a secular state such as Nigeria. During the transition period, leaders of both communities argued heatedly for and against its inclusion in the new Constitution. On the one hand, Muslim leaders have insisted that removing the provision for Sharia from the Constitution would "destroy the country," and Christians, on the other hand, have declared that all references to Muslim law must be removed. In the end, framers of the 1999 Constitution seem to have settled for much the same careful wording as in the 1979 Constitution, allowing for the application of Islamic civil law only when all parties involved are Muslim.

Another divisive issue is the ambiguous status of Nigeria's membership in the Organization of the Islamic Conference (OIC). The government tries to ignore implications of participation in OIC meetings out of deference to the passions aroused in the Christian community over the perceived implication that Nigeria is a Muslim state.

A number of local efforts to achieve peace between Muslims and Christians indicates a growing awareness of the importance of cooperation among religious groups. These attempts include the creation of "peace teams" at the Center for Peace Research and Conflict Resolution in 1996 at the National War College in Abuja and several universities. Whether or not these efforts have had any success is difficult to judge at present, but the fact that they are being made by the government and universities probably indicates that both civilian and military elites see their future well-being linked to better intercommunal relations.

The election of a Christian southerner as president in Nigeria, which has been dominated politically by northerners since the last century, is a notable breakthrough. That he achieved office with the support of northern Muslims is yet another. Moreover, that Christians and Muslims were able to work together to bring this event about would not have been predicted less than a year ago. This confluence of events points to both fundamental changes taking place in the Muslim community and to the possibility of a new configuration of politics in the Nigerian federation.

However, the continuance of the present national Muslim-Christian entente depends in part on the political adroitness with which the new government manages the problems besetting the Muslim community and whether it can extend the power-sharing agreement to regional and local levels. Still, it will be difficult to accomplish this without strong Muslim leadership at the national level. However, elements of each community see the political behind the religious whenever points of contention arise. Thus, there have been numerous precedents for the latest round of violence.

Religious issues dominated the political scene through the late 1970s and the 1980s, but until the late 1980s, Muslim-Christian violence was rare. It emerged early in the 1980s after the formation of "Shia" groups in northern universities that painted "Islam only" on campus walls, particularly at Ahmadu Bello University and Bayero University in Kano. In October 1982, the Kano group marched to the Sabon Gari, Kano's predominantly Christian district, and burned several churches.[62]

Throughout the 1980s and early 1990s, Muslim-Christian violence was responsible for many of Nigeria's more than 5,000 casualties in communal fighting. Typical was the outbreak of rioting in Kano in the early 1990s over the arrival of a proselytizing European preacher to hold large public meetings; a visiting Muslim preacher had been denied similar privileges.

The violence, said to have been the worst in a decade, resulted in more than 300 deaths and extensive property damage. But it was soon over-shadowed by yearly religious outbursts that took hundreds of lives in northern and central states. Religious clashes continued sporadically. On October 13, 2001, more than 100 persons were reported dead in Muslim-Christian encounters in Kano, following a Muslim demonstration to pro-test the bombing of Afghanistan by the United States.[63] After similar riots in Jos, the Anglican archbishop of Nigeria first expressed condo-lences to Americans for the loss of life on September 11, then issued a press release stating, "It is worth noting that the excesses of religious fundamentalists are evident even in Nigeria where you have wanton de-struction of life and property every now and then by those who arrogate to themselves the responsibility of fighting the cause of God."[64]

In early 1986, press reports revealed that the Babangida government had secretly upgraded its observer status in the OIC to full membership—without discussion even within leadership circles. At the same time, mem-bers of the northern establishment urged the government to make Sharia courts available to Muslims in the South. The issue landed on the front pages of the government press, throwing the country into a firestorm of religious controversy. The Christian community considered the OIC the in-club of Muslim states, and the spread of Muslim law to the South as clear signals that the country's Muslim leaders were turning Nigeria into a Muslim theocracy. The uneasy but until then stable relationship be-tween the religious communities was undercut, and Christians in both northern and southern regions drew together against the Muslim majority in the North.[65]

By the spring of 1987, all that was needed was a spark to set off a confrontation of unprecedented violence between Muslims and Chris-tians. A minor doctrinal dispute—a Christian minister was alleged to have misrepresented the Koran in his preaching—raised the wrath of Muslim Brotherhood members who were students at Kafanchan College of Education. Violence escalated throughout cities in the state of Kaduna; spread to the neighboring state of Kano, where Christian churches and businesses, as well as mosques, were destroyed; and in the end left over 100 dead and approximately $1.5 million of property destroyed.[66] Eyewit-nesses described a devastating tidal wave of "rioting, looting, killing, and burning . . . of vehicles, homes, mosques and churches. It took nearly two weeks to bring the situation under control and by the time the police restored order, the scope of the destruction left many Nigerians bewildered over what it had all been about."[67]

"Sharia: Our Pride, Their Fear"

For non-Muslim westerners, one of the most puzzling aspects of contemporary Islamic political theory is its insistence on religion as the defining principle of public life. This goes against the fundamental commitment to separation of church and state, the legacy of Western Enlightenment thinking about the sovereignty of the secular state. Islam unites philosophy and policy, believing that physical and spiritual existence, temporal and secular authority, and science and faith are one.[68] The underlying debate over secular versus religious law that undergirds much of the disagreement over the application of the Sharia was exemplified in the great Sharia debate of 1977–1978 and its results on the 1979 Constitution.[69] The Western concept that religion is largely a private, as opposed to a public, issue and "should not be allowed to have any direct role or influence on the public life of the people"[70] is the basis of secularism that many Muslims reject.

In 1986, Babangida amended the 1979 Constitution, removing the restriction of Sharia to personal law, which had limited its applicability to civil law, thus opening it up to criminal matters—which had been specifically rejected in the long Sharia debate of 1977–1978. With hindsight, Christians in the year 2000 saw this as part of a calculated single process, leading through the drafting of the 1979 Constitution and its 1986 and 1999 successors.[71] The introduction of Sharia legislation in Zamfara in 1999 was quickly added to the roster of conspiratorial acts aimed at Islamizing the country. The Christian Association of Nigeria (CAN) offered legal aid to Malam Buba Jangedi after President Obasanjo suggested that he seek legal redress if he wished. It had been argued that only a legal challenge to the Sharia initiated by someone whose human rights had been violated would have a chance in Nigerian courts of challenging its constitutionality.[72]

If the amputation issue symbolized the distance between radical Muslim and Christian points of view, the violent reaction it provoked shortly in the neighboring state of Kaduna struck an ominous note for Nigerians committed to the country's continued unity. When the governor of Kaduna shortly afterward proposed introducing the Sharia soon, Christians marched in protest against the proposal, and a battle erupted with a mob of youthful pro-Sharia Muslims. Within days, over a thousand deaths and injuries ensued, as well as several million dollars in property damage. The conflict left a trail of graffiti throughout the city both in support of and against Sharia, depending on the quarter. Press reports said that the city was divided as Beirut once was, with a river running between Muslims to the north and Christians to the south.[73]

In a somber speech to the country, President Obasanjo declared that the conflict was the most destructive act in Nigerian life since the 1967–1970 Civil War. The Kaduna riots were followed by ripple effects else-where. Thousands more non-Muslim southerners fled their businesses and homes in the North, seeking refuge at police and military barracks from the surrounding Muslim community's rage; many returned to the South, hoping for protection in their homelands. Despite reassuring words from northern officials, the violence continued, spreading to the northeastern state of Borno, where traditional leaders had vowed it would not occur.

The Zamfara bombshell took the Sharia issue into another dimension. The administration of justice is one of the most important functions of any Muslim government and an essential element in the definition of the Muslim community. Previously, Muslims in Nigeria's North had access to the Sharia through area courts for issues of family law, such as inheritance rights. However, the new law extended the Sharia into areas that reflected the pressures and conditions of the modern world, such as abuses of the law by public servants, forgery, criminal misappropriation of property, and breach of trust by bank officials or merchants.

At independence, non-Muslims were loath to accept jurisdiction of the Muslim courts when (1) evidence given by Muslim males outweighed that of a woman, a Christian, or a pagan (a Muslim man would be let off if he swore his innocence); (2) different rates of monetary penalties for homicide were applied according to the victim's religion; and (3) the traditionalist emirs still controlled the courts. Furthermore, the Penal Code of 1960 incorporated some principles of Islamic law—notably, crim-inalizing adultery and fornication outside of marriage; criminalizing con-sumption of alcohol; and applying punishment by lashing, as prescribed by the Sharia, which non-Muslims found repugnant.[74]

Nor were Muslims content with the arrangement. They criticized the courts' corruption and inefficiency and the judges' lack of legal training. In the eyes of Muslim scholars, application of Sharia stagnated during the colonial period as its emphasis moved from social relevance and pub-lic good to modernizations that would bring it into line with Western ju-risprudence. There was a growing tendency in Islamic courts to follow British rules of precedence, rather than sticking to the traditional sources of Sharia, especially the Koran and Hadith (traditions of the Prophet).[75] Moreover, the British colonial administration applied a "repugnancy doc-trine," discarding provisions such as amputation that the British believed were "repugnant to natural justice, equity, and good conscience."[76] Muslims found the definition of the Sharia as "native law and custom" denigrating and complained that although some 40% of Yoruba living in the South and in Lagos were Muslim, Islamic law has never been applied to them.[77]

Since independence, Islamic judges in Nigeria have been exercising the now popular function of *ijtihad*—or independent reasoning in interpretation of Sharia—as they apply the law "as an instrument of social engineering to meet the challenges of the contemporary world."[78]

The framers of Nigeria's 1979 Constitution, the principles of which are preserved virtually intact in the 1999 Constitution, drew their inspiration from European and American secularism rather than from the constitutional principles applied by Muslim states in the North (Borno and Sokoto) since the beginning of the nineteenth century. The constitutionalists saw Islam as a historical accident that had become a "spent force."[79] As a result of the success of this point of view, Sharia was recognized as one of three systems of law, which included English common law and customary law, and its jurisdiction was constitutionally reduced to the law of personal status (marriage, divorce, inheritance, etc.).[80]

The Muslim community insisted on a Federal Sharia Court of Appeal, though agreeing as well to a Supreme Court that would apply "English" law. Christians launched a storm of protest, insisting that this put the law in Nigeria on a dual track and was again a step in the direction of an Islamic republic. Some Muslim jurists responded in the heat of debate by publicly questioning the value of continuing the common law and called for a total restructuring of the legal system.[81] However, moderates on both sides again prevailed and supported a hierarchy of appeals courts, including Sharia Courts of Appeal, a Federal Court of Appeal, and a Supreme Court whose judges were expected to be learned in Islamic, as well as common, law.[82] The appeals issue was revived in the constitutional debates in 1989 with equal passion. However, both the Constitutions of 1989 and 1999 left the 1979 compromise in place, although the framers in 1999 limited the Sharia Appeals Court to cases involving personal law only—the narrowest interpretation yet. So little attention was paid to the issue at the time that observers predicted that controversy over the Sharia had finally been laid to rest. Instead, the great Sharia debate of 2000 moved out of federal jurisdiction and into that of the northern state governments.[83]

Why Now?

From independence on, the potential for quarreling over the law has been in place, a ready issue for earlier generations of leaders who saw the possibility of tearing apart Nigeria's disparate communities. Also, Muslims were increasingly disillusioned with the way in which postcolonial assets were distributed in Nigeria, where a small percentage of persons at the top, many of them Muslims, had grabbed the lion's share of Nigeria's wealth. The rest of the country is still struggling to wrest a meaningful and dignified living out of the thin leavings that remain. Nigeria's increasingly difficult economic, social, and political environment has particularly struck the Muslim North—despite the fact that most recent national governments have been dominated by northern politicians and military. Strands of economic and political frustrations and societal dislocation are woven through religious issues. Clearly, a sense of citizenship has been lacking in the elites' approaches to development. There has been little evidence of turning back profits to enrich the country's human environment. Adam Smith's perception of civic greed, of an arrogant minority taking everything and controlling the fate of the majority, appears particularly applicable to Nigeria.[84] Nearly a half-century of independence seems to impoverished Muslim residents of Nigeria's North to have alleviated colonial exploitation to a negligible extent. For such people the rhetoric of democratization and capitalist development resonates as hollowly as the worn-out phrases of international socialism.

The vast majority of Nigerians—70%, or 77 million people—live below the poverty line, with over 23% destitute, most of them in the North. Northern Muslims believe that one of the causes of radical Muslim reform in Nigeria was the imposition of the government's Structural Adjustment Programme (SAP), which contributed to the collapse of living standards and to an economic crisis. The subsequent suffering of the public majority caused them to seek their own solutions to their economic plight, using Muslim identity as an important factor in mobilizing public resistance. Where marginalized communities were divided both ethnically and religiously, this division became a rallying cry for violence—in Kafanchan, Zangonn-Kataf, and Tafawa Balewa and on a regular basis in Kaduna and Kano. Disputes, often worded in terms of religious differences, also centered on class divisions, the power of traditional Hausa-Fulani leadership, access to economic resources, and the belief of long-established Christian communities that the Hausa-Fulani has usurped their land.[85]

As with most poor nations, Nigeria has no safety-net programs.[86] Excesses of neglect and corruption since independence have become features of popular culture. Fuel distribution breakdowns in this major oil-producing state and a member of the Organization of Oil Exporting Countries (OPEC) create daily, hours-long lines at gas stations. Unemployment remains high.

Zamfara itself, in the near desert environment of the far North, has a heavily troubled economy, although blessed with resources—it has the country's second-largest gold deposits and a quarter of Nigeria's hides and skins, and it is the third-largest producer of cotton and second-largest producer of tobacco and peanuts. However, there is no potable water in the capital city, Gusau; there are fewer than 20 secondary schools in the state; and Zamfara is among the most backward places in education in the country.[87]

At independence, Nigeria's national leaders, most of whom were northern Muslims, opted for a secular, democratic model of government; a presidential system; and a capitalist economy—all of which soon entered a downward spiral of military coups and authoritarian rule, with intermittent attempts to form civilian governments.

In the process, the budding middle class was decimated, and a traditional northern elite, empowered in National Politics failed to see the need to develop its northern constituency. Of the billions of *naira* that have been plundered from the state, little was returned to the Muslim North. After the Zamfara amputation, there were calls for the sentence to be applied to the top levels of corrupt officialdom, chief of which was the family of the former military dictator, Sani Abacha, who is believed to have stolen a record billions of dollars.

The latest round of corruption—and the recorded worst—took place during the transition to democracy in 1999 during the administration of General Abdulsalami Abubakar. The presidency alone let out 4,072 contracts in 5 months, most of them illegal, and causing "huge financial and administrative havoc," according to a commission of inquiry. As a result, although Nigeria had long been mired in corrupt practices, the commission found that public service standards "had collapsed and discipline was almost completely banished from the system."[88] As a result, a gulf has widened between rich and poor within the Muslim community, as well as in the rest of the country. Government meddling has embroiled the community in internecine quarrels that have weakened it and at the same time have encouraged aggressive behavior.

After hopes had been raised by the election of Nigeria's first southern, Christian head of state, bringing Nigeria from military rule to civilian-controlled democracy, the Obesanjo government's honeymoon a year later had run its course. The northern population—elites and the grassroots—

that supported him and formed the core of his electoral victory became impatient for good results. Despite early dismissal of military and others on the make throughout the previous military administration and transitional government, graft and corruption seem largely unchecked. In this highly centralized system of political benefits, northern Muslims felt themselves marginalized from the centers of power and profit. They believed that this Southern Baptist president, a graduate of long years in prison, during which he was isolated from the flow of national politics, had surrounded himself with like-minded cronies, equally out of touch with the community's needs.

Muslims were particularly angry over the state of the judicial system and breakdown of law and order that left the rank and file vulnerable to the venality of judges and long court delays. The oft-heard complaint was that justice delayed was justice denied.

As Ali Ameer writes, "The issue, which in the final analysis will determine the future strength and legitimacy of the Islamists is economic. Unless the economic welfare of a majority of Muslims improves, Islamism and its appeal for a religious alternative will remain vibrant." For the present they are "caught in a *global trap* in which fewer and fewer get richer and richer, more and more get impoverished and the inequality gets consolidated."[89]

As people of all ethnic backgrounds indigenous to the region have dispersed throughout the federal republic, traditional identities and ties have weakened. Those of family, locality, and ethnic group no longer provide the primary identification, as in the past. For example, facial scarification once identified a person's place of origin, but that is no longer so. Even such a distinctive Nigerian indicator as dress can no longer be counted on to telegraph where its wearer originated. "Show me a Nigerian, and I will tell you where he comes from by what he wears," a Nigerian customs official once remarked.[90] For example, a hand-sewn huntsman's hat, long a badge of a Hausa, has been adopted by some Yoruba, who produce the headwear with rough machine stitching, indicating it is for regular wear and no longer the distinctive headgear of a northern hunter. Intermarriage is increasingly common, and in some interfaith marriages the wife goes to church and the husband to a mosque; but Muslim women are forbidden to marry outside the faith and children go with the Muslim man.

Disillusionment with the West is also widespread, some of it based on films, television, and the popular press. Recently, one thoughtful northern Muslim who had visited the United States on a Leader Grant reported his preconception of America as a gun-toting society where extreme violence was the norm. This perception had been formed by the film industry and the media.[91]

In such a fluid social climate, it is easier than ever to rally youthful activists on all sides of an issue. Elders find themselves unable to control the undereducated, unemployed youths of the Muslim community, especially those with ample time on their hands and a quest for any form of excitement.

Islam lends itself to the spirit of protest and reform that Nigerian Muslims are articulating in the Sharia movement. Nigerian Muslims remember Islam's protest against "Arabian tribalism and Meccan plutocracy"[92] in the seventh century, as well as the traditions of Nigeria's own victorious reforms of the nineteenth century. They hope that through the Sharia they can again recapture the sense of power and legitimacy that characterized those earlier movements. In a troubled present, the real or imagined stability of a golden past becomes an attraction against which unsettled times are measured and found wanting.

Aftershocks

As usually happens in Nigeria, the original communal quarrel soon broadened to a more general political question. There have been calls for a reconfiguration of states into six regional units with considerable local autonomy, raising concerns for the continued unity of the country. Of the six units, four have strong Muslim components or ties:

- The Hausa-speaking Northwest, consisting of Sokoto and its neighboring conservative Muslim states
- The Northeast cluster centered on Borno, which has followed an independent political line from Sokoto domination since the nineteenth century
- The North Central states, which incorporate strong Muslim minorities
- The Southeast region, with its Christian majority, which with the notable exception of the 1960s Biafra war has cooperated with the Muslim North since independence
- The oil-producing, Christian southern states, which have also cooperated politically with the North in the past
- The Southwest Yoruba states, which since the nineteenth century have been nearly evenly divided between Muslims and Christians

The allocation of senior positions in the new government across religious and regional lines has been critically important in keeping all sections of the country in support of the president. Such a divide-and-conquer strategy has been widely used by African leaders; every important ethnic constituency is represented, although none is fully happy; and when the protest levels suggest that the delicate balance is askew, it is realigned again, to await a reshuffling.

Under pressure from the central government, the 19 "northern" governors met with the National Council of State in April 2000 and agreed for the time being to hold off implementation of the Sharia penal code. Governors from the far northern states later vowed not to repeal the Sharia legislation already passed by state assemblies.[93] The judicial panel of inquiry probing the Kaduna Sharia crisis heard testimony that irreconcilable differences between the Hausa-Fulani, who dominate the state government and its economy, and their southern Kaduna counterparts made it imperative to split the state in two, leaving the Muslims in control of the northern segment and Christian southerners in control of the South.[94] Meanwhile, cracks appeared in the 40-year alliance of Middle Belt states with those in the far North.[95] In the wake of the Sharia crisis, Middle Belt spokesmen complained that "the South misunderstands us, the North rejects us."[96]

The southern-based press has trumpeted a conspiratorial explanation of the whole Sharia issue. Accusations in the Lagos press are echoed by many observers in both North and South, claiming that the issue is the creation of the long-established, northern, Hausa-Fulani elite, which since the beginning of the nineteenth century has dominated regional politics but now feels threatened by the Obesanjo regime. This opinion alleges that the Sharia issue has been fabricated in order to undermine the regime through civil unrest. Let the country show itself ungovernable by Christian southerners, and the northern military can again intervene—so this line of reasoning goes.

To ward off such a development, the regime has transferred officers and dispersed military units, moving them out of proximity to the major centers of power—hoping that the availability of military support for a coup from Dodon Barracks, outside of Lagos, traditional launching point for such activities, would thus be blocked.

Meanwhile, Governor Sani announced that the Sharia issue was nonnegotiable, and the public in Zamfara appeared to be giving him solid support. The headmaster of an Izala school in Gusau stated that the public was solidly behind Sharia,[97] and northern observers said that support for

Sharia came from the grassroots of disillusioned northerners wanting jobs and a wider distribution of financial resources. It also gained popularity because of the anger and frustration northerners felt with the graft-ridden, foot-dragging pace of Nigeria's common law legal system. The politician who first grasped the movement's political potential—Governor Sani of Zamfara—became the man of the hour in the early months of 2000, a popular hero to the furiously disappointed masses of the North's dispossessed youths, some of whom call themselves "Sani boys." Whatever doubts traditional leaders, economic elites, and intellectuals might have had about Governor Sani's rough-and-ready approach to this explosive issue of social change, they quickly went on record as supporting his move. In the absence of published statistics, there was soon a widespread belief that crime rates in Zamfara had plunged since the amputation.[98]

Reaffirmation of the country's unity in its present federal form came from many sources. However, every position taken politically in Nigeria seems to call forth its opposite. It is axiomatic in postindependence Nigerian politics that one regional initiative will bring forth an equally strongly advocated proposal from another region that will neutralize the first. With equal passion, the governors of the southeastern states announced support for a confederal rather than federal system, which would allow considerable autonomy for six regional units, and urged holding a Nigeria-wide conference, presumably to settle outstanding Muslim-Christian issues on a national basis.[99]

Beyond the screaming headlines, a stab at dialogue was attempted in Zamfara, where a pan-Nigerian group of elders met with the governor.[100] Also, the National Council of State met with the northern governors to discuss the Sharia crisis, and the governors agreed to suspend implementation of the Islamic criminal code. They read a statement afterward that the North would downplay implementation—although the body language of several governors made clear their opposition. Two former heads of state—Alhaji Shehu Shagari and Major General Muhamadu Buhari—criticized any suspension of Sharia criminal laws, further inflaming passions in the Christian community. Soon several of the northern governors rescinded any moderate, middle positions on the issue of implementation. Alhaji Umaru Shinkafi, head of the All Peoples Party (APP) and formerly chief of the National Security Organization (NSO), vowed that it was too late to cancel the application of the Sharia provisions and urged the application of Sharia in the South as well. As already stated, Governor Sani vowed that Sharia was nonnegotiable.[101]

As indicators of narrow ethnic identities fade with new generations, an increasingly vocal Christian community sharpens Muslims' sense of corporate unity, continuing to clarify Muslim identity and provide a means by which the community can react to changes in the contemporary world, many of them seen as threatening. Identification with a specific, all-encompassing, religiously based system of law that is not shared with other groups in the country also confirms group identity and tends to erase internal fissures. Over the past 30 years, the community had been riven by internal conflict over what it is to be a "good Muslim." In the 1980s this played out in the conflict with the followers of Marwa.

At the same time, Nigerian Muslims' participation in the yearly pilgrimage (hajj) to Mecca, while exposing the community to issues of global Islam, has also been shown to strengthen Nigerians' sense of their own membership in a national Muslim community. Abubakar Gumi, contemptuous of Nigerians who arrived in Mecca and were ignorant of correct forms of worship in executing the hajj, set off the wider Izala-Darkika conflict of the 1980s over what it meant to be a good Muslim. The Sharia controversy seems to have helped to quiet the long-simmering quarrels between Izala and Darika traditionalists.

Gumi's 1992 death came at a time when leadership in the northern Muslim community was undergoing a sweeping generational change. Older leaders, who had run things since independence, were ill or dead. The northern Muslim community, as with the rest of the country, was reeling under the oppressive rule of General Abacha, who was unwilling to tolerate competing sources of power. Ibrahim Dasuki, the former businessman whom the military had installed as sultan of Sokoto to lead the national Muslim community, was now viewed as a threat and removed from office in 1996. The elderly Muslim leader installed in his place, Muhammadu Maccido, was unable to challenge the Abacha regime to a similar extent.[102]

Gumi's nationwide movement, the Izala, was breaking up into groups led by less charismatic men. A younger generation of dissatisfied Muslims was coalescing under the leadership of Ibrahim Zak Zaky, who though in prison for undisclosed charges, was attracting an exponentially expanding following with his call for Muslim reform and total reorganization of the state to fit an Iranian-style theocratic model. He soon became the only voice of opposition against the Abacha regime. Since his release from prison, the movement's rise has been less spectacular. Moreover, not anxious to enter the current political maelstrom, Zak Zaky has distanced himself from the Sharia proponents.

Outlook for the Future

The contentious relations between Muslims and Christians in recent years made results of the 1999 presidential election hopeful for those wishing Nigeria's religious communities could bury their animosities. Nigeria's president is a Christian, a born-again Baptist, a Yoruba from the South, elected unexpectedly by the grassroots population of the Muslim North.

The political mood of the North since Obasanjo's election appeared optimistic for the first time in many years. The economy and morale have begun to show some hesitant signs of life in the wake of Abacha's death— a 50% increase in the price of oil, the success of the democratic elections, and the release of political prisoners. This in turn gave Obasanjo a window of opportunity to engage in a government reform and democratization program without ongoing fighting between faith-based groups. It also provided him with a reservoir of support in the North, which a Christian Yoruba could not have enjoyed in the past.

However, communal disputes still simmer near the surface, the military lacks an apolitical tradition, and the government is financially broke to begin with. Thus, the future, in which Muslim-Christian differences will test the government's resolve and skills in their own way, seems uncertain and likely to remain so.

If the government fails to reverse Nigeria's economic decline, it is also questionable whether the leadership of religious communities can overcome geographic, ethnic, and class differences. With so many Muslim school-leavers and university graduates with little chance for employment, Islamic activism could provide the means of achieving influence and economic advancement if traditional leadership lacks the drive or resources to fill the existing vacuum. And if the economy does not improve or Obasanjo's transition to democracy falters, violence between the two communities is likely to continue.

However, with each religious conflict between Muslims and Christians, religious identity moves up the scale of importance. Thus, for many inhabitants of a northern state, there are two kinds of human beings— Muslims and Christians. And on this consideration most other forms of relationships are forged, such as allegiance to a region, ethnic group, or extended family. This notion of religious solidarity becomes more reinforced with the passing of each religious and ethnic dispute, and since 1987 there have been eight major religious or ethnic feuds, each more costly in human and material casualties than the last. Predictably, churches and mosques are the first victims of attacks by Muslim and

Christian youth gangs. The religious issue is bound up in ethnic and economic contrasts as well. Igbos—who feel themselves victimized in the North in a pogrom—resent the Muslims' "prolonged monopoly of power" and economic advantages, including fixed prices for fertilizers and food crops, government contracts, and jobs. Christian residents of northern states assert that to attain any top job there, the most important criterion is religion, followed by ethnicity, with qualifications and experience coming last. Christians resent this, and "Muslims resent the Christians for resenting them."[103]

By May 2000, though Sharia legislation was being passed in the North, many observers believed that the Sharia group was lying low for the present and would not implement the laws. In the words of Philip Ostien, "It is clear that Nigerians, not only in the North, have a fair amount of unfinished business still to transact in relation to the court systems . . . and the Area courts in particular."[104] These courts symbolize the cluster of problems facing the Muslim community in the contemporary world. Muslims both advocate Islamic law and broaden its application despite non-Muslim convictions that the Sharia is an instrument of oppression and a thinly veiled effort to Islamize the country.[105]

One of the attractions at the grassroots level of the Sharia movement is the promise that the Muslim requirement of *zakat*—the sharing of wealth—will be enforced. This is fueled by near universal frustration that one of Africa's countries with the richest potential has tumbled to the status of a Third World basket case. An oft-repeated theme of the current head of state is that the world is looking to Nigeria as an example of what can be done on the African continent.

To many observers, the frequent hammer blows of demonstrations and violence associated with movements for Islamic reform show clear signs of a revolt of an underclass desperate for "respect and a job," in the words of one Kanuri *mallam*. Religious demonstrations usually end in wholesale looting of small businesses and destruction of property, but with few positive results.[106]

It would not be difficult for talented Nigerian jurists to design a legal system incorporating both aspects of Sharia and common law and to include the traditional law of other regions in local courts that deal with family and commercial issues. But the difficulty is that the law is so inextricably tied to religion in Nigerian Islam, and as tensions within Nigeria mount, the gulf between haves and have-nots widens, arms become increasingly available, ideological positions harden, and possibilities for intelligent compromise and dialogue diminish. It is the eleventh hour, and a strong governmental effort at mediation could help diffuse the climate, as could an upturn in the economy and a sustained effort at goodwill and cooperation by Muslim and Christian leaders. No such positive forces appear on the horizon at this point, but Nigerians in the past have headed for the brink and then pulled back. Without such a turning point, the future is not hopeful.

Islam in the Sudan

Moving Beyond the Crossroads?

As the only state in sub-Saharan Africa whose political structures are built on Islamic law and constitution, Muslim Sudan is entering an exceptionally fluid period in its history. During the postindependence era, it suffered from destructive competition among sectarian Islamic groups and their political parties that paralyzed the decision-making process during periods of civilian rule. For the past 10 years a heavy-handed Islamic government has made policy by employing the mind-set of a beleaguered, vulnerable state beset by non-Muslim "enemies" within and without, often at a heavy human cost. The imposition of a draconian version of Islamic law has become the symbol of Muslim-Christian conflict in Africa. However, at present there are indications that the authoritarian Sudanese regime is moving tentatively in a more pragmatic and democratic direction as the postindependence era fades and a new generation of potential leaders emerges:

- The government is opening up the electoral process, and formerly banned political parties are forming and being licensed. The opposition Umma Party in exile has signed an agreement with the Khartoum government that could open the way for the reinstatement of a meaningful dialogue.
- The Islamic regime is moving toward concrete efforts to settle long-standing issues with its neighbors and the West, despite pressures from abroad that have played into the hands of hard-liners

who oppose change. If, as some observers believe, Sudan's Islamic ideological leader, Hasan al-Turabi, has been permanently moved to the sidelines, government policies unacceptable to the West are likely to moderate more rapidly, especially in the aftermath of the September 11, 2001, events. Nevertheless, under the best of circumstances, it will take time for democratic institutions representing Sudan's pluralistic society to emerge from this cautious Islamic government.

• Khartoum is again attempting to convince all faction leaders in the South to accept a solution to Sudan's long-standing civil war that would still allow the North to retain an Islamic government. For this to happen, it will require leadership in both the North and South that is capable of producing a durable peace, grappling with Sudan's grave economic problems, and finding some modification of the present Islamic legal system to fit the requirements of a pluralistic state.

An Islamic political system is clearly here to stay in Sudan, and solutions that ignore this fact will remain empty exercises. The majority of the Sudan's population, if allowed to express its wishes democratically, remains committed to maintaining Islamic societal and political principles as the foundation of the modern Sudanese state. If given a democratic option, state and society will continue to be modeled on Islamic law but will probably move in a more inclusive, representative direction.

Detracting from this process are the many northern politicians who use religion under the guise of espousing Islamic purity to consolidate their own political position. They continue to ignore what numerous other countries have discovered, that a federalist political-legal system can accommodate pluralistic views. In short, successful politics is the art of compromise, and religious purists remain uncompromising. Political Islam can move only a limited distance toward effectively organizing a modern state; in Sudan's case, it cannot provide a much-needed national identity but only a component of it.[1]

Geography and History: The Bilad al-Sudan

Sudan represents a crossroads between Africa and the Arab world, between North and sub-Saharan Africa. An immense, largely barren country with a Muslim North, home to numerous factions and brotherhoods, and a largely Christian South, where hundreds of distinct languages are spoken and as many different ethnic groups live,[2] it is a state where long-feuding groups can severely damage one another but never provide the knockout punch. A brief survey of Sudan's history indicates how such a contradictory state of affairs emerged, for Sudan is a country where geography and history directly influence contemporary behavior.

The territory that constitutes the present-day Republic of the Sudan is nearly 1 million square miles, roughly a quarter of the size of Europe, with a population of perhaps 34 million. Most of the land is barren and rocky, semidesert or savanna, with some rainlands and highlands to the south. The Nile flows northward from Khartoum, but land in agricultural use is rare, with the exception of the Gezira Peninsula between the Blue and White Niles, where formerly grain and now cotton is grown.[3] The Sudan is a country where large areas have the potential for agricultural use if properly managed. The range areas of middle Dar Fur and Kordofan are potentially excellent places for herding and mixed farming, and the same is true of parts of eastern Sudan. Likewise, there are large tracts elsewhere where rain-fed agriculture would be possible. Some of the problems of desertification are caused by humans, and Sudan has tried various large-scale agricultural development schemes that remain case studies in what not to do in developmental planning. John O. Voll has noted, "In the 1970s, people were making a good case for the possibility of Sudan being the 'breadbasket' of the Arab world. That vision failed because of human failure, not the lack of natural resources."[4]

The term *Bilad al-Sudan*, "the land of the blacks," is used to describe the land south of Egypt, which was connected through trade routes to Egypt and the Red Sea, although other such routes spread out in different directions as well. Along such arteries pilgrims made their way to Mecca, often taking several years and sometimes supporting their lengthy journeys by begging or manual laborer. Conversely, Muslim scholars and missionaries traveled to what is now the Sudan and gradually established a strong Muslim presence.

As might be expected, given its proximity to Egypt, the Sudan's North is largely an Arabic-speaking Muslim land, although a minority of long-established Arabic-speaking Christians reside there as well. Arabic ancestry is a source of pride to an Islamic northerner, and lengthy pedigrees trace descent to early Arab families. A distinctive feature of Islam in Sudan is the prevalence of numerous Sufi "holy families," who remain relatively independent of the political process but whose ancestral tombs are frequently visited by followers of local teacher-leaders.[5]

Southern Sudan, politically, ethnically, and religiously, stands in stark contrast to the North. It is home to numerous linguistic and ethnic

groups, and it is here that Christian missionaries were successful in converting large numbers of people, especially since the nineteenth century.
Although there has been some Islamization in the South, most southerners do not claim Arabic descent. The cattle-raising Nuer and the Azande,
whose lands are now divided by the Sudan-Zaire border, are among the
best known of the southern peoples.

During much of the nineteenth century the Sudan came under Turco-
Egyptian suzerainty and was a modest source of gold and, more extensively, of slaves (some of whom were trained as soldiers for the Egyptian
army), as well as high tax revenues—up to $15 per slave and $10 a cow.[6]
Sporadic, leaderless revolts flared up in response to harsh taxation, especially in villages along the Nile, but were eventually put down by the
numerically superior Egyptians. What followed was a time of stagnation
and a climate of resentment toward the northern invaders. Notable was
the reign of Khedive Isma'il, 1863–1881, which considerably increased
the territories held by Egypt, suppressed the slave trade at the instigation
of westerners, and imported numerous Europeans for trusted positions in
the civil and military administrations.

Isma'il was deposed in 1879. His reign was a time of unfilled grandiose
schemes—a railway project that would link Sudan with Egypt but went
only a few miles, a rail and river transport company that went bankrupt
after promising economic prosperity, and a vast cotton-growing enterprise
that was never successful. These were the first of a succession of developmental schemes that have plagued Sudan's economic life, promising
much but delivering little. Their importance to this narrative is that they
helped disillusion the Sudanese rank and file, and later the intelligensia,
with the perceived failures of Western technology and material culture, a
theme that Islamic fundamentalist preachers would later exploit with considerable success.

The Mahdi

Into a world of infidelity and unbelief came the Mahdi. It is not that
things were simmering, waiting for revolt. The Sudan had been under
foreign control for 60 years, but not until the collapse of the khedivate
in 1879 was it possible to make a move that might succeed. From the
island of Aba in the White Nile came a series of letters to officials in
various parts of the Sudan, telling them that the Expected Mahdi had
arrived. Beginning in 1881, Muhammad Ahmad ibn 'Abdallah, a 40-year-
old ascetic with a reputation for holiness and supernatural powers, an-

nounced publicly that he was the one appointed by Allah to bring in a reign of justice and equity with the approach of the eschaton. Trained by local teachers, the Mahdi was a member of the Sammaniyya order, an offshoot of the eighteenth-century revival and reform movement.[7]

Modern Sudanese commentators have attempted to call Muhammad Ahmad "the Father of Independence," but nothing in his life or teachings was associated with any idea of nationalism. Instead, the Mahdi's teachings established a precedent for an Islamic tradition of rule rather than a modern nation-state.[8] The Mahdi, supported by a growing band of followers, took on the titles of imam, the leader of the Muslim community, and successor of the apostle of God, the one who would usher in the new age. Initially, he attracted the discontented and marginalized in society. Specifically, his appeal was to nomads who sought to "kill the Turks and cease to pay taxes," pious bled-dwellers—those who lived in the vast rural areas—who yearned for Islam to be the rule by which their land was governed, and the community of Nile boatmen and slave traders who had lost their lucrative livelihood and were willing to give religious language to what were really economic motives "since the institution of slavery was not as such repugnant to Islam."[9]

Several military victories in 1882 and 1883 by the Mahdi propelled his forces into prominence. Meanwhile, the energetic British leader Governor-General Charles Gordon returned with orders from London to survey plans for an evacuation. Instead, and acting on his own, Gordon announced his intention to "smash the Mahdi," something his meager forces would not allow. On October 32, 1884, the Mahdi besieged Khartoum and attacked on January 26, 1885, killing Gordon and taking the city. However, for rural, ascetic Muhammad Ahmad, the city meant little, and he pressed his campaign elsewhere in the countryside until his premature death of typhus that June 22.[10]

The Mahdi's plans for a postconquest state were very much a work in progress at his death. His goal and that of his Ansar, or "companions of the Prophet," was nothing less than the restoration of primitive Islam, the return to what he and other visionaries in comparable settings believed was a golden age. He appointed administrators as successors to the three caliphs named by the Prophet to command the Muslim armies. A tax collector and chief judge were added to their numbers, but the administrative system never took hold. A power struggle followed the Mahdi's death; his allies fell on one another, and a piecemeal regime stayed in place until an Anglo-Egyptian condominium was installed in 1899.

The Condominium, 1899–1956

The hybrid form of government by which the Sudan was ruled from 1899 to 1956 was called a condominium. Egyptian and British flags were flown jointly throughout the Sudan, but it was the British governor-general who ruled by decree; and since the Sudan was not a colony, his instructions came from the Foreign Office, not the Colonial Office. The ultimate effect of this system was dissatisfaction for all parties—the British because their budget must be passed and funds raised from the Egyptian government; the Egyptians because they regarded the condominium scheme as a sham; and the Sudanese, especially when nationalistic voices emerged in the 1920s, because they were ruled by foreign powers.

The new government's first task was pacification. Following the Mahdi's death, several followers continued to resist the Anglo-Egyptian presence, and self-declared Madhis appeared periodically in the desert, alarming the British, who quickly rushed out to suppress them. In extending the British presence, the governor-general was aided by a remarkable individual, Slatin Pasha, nominally inspector-general of tribal and religious affairs, but who had free reign to intervene in all aspects of the administration until World War I, when he was forced to resign since he was an Austrian national.[11] Paternalism was a feature of British administration, and close bonds developed among the Sudan administrators, many of whom spent long careers there. A British newspaper described them as "athletic public school boys accustomed to hard work rather than hard thinking,"[12] and for many the nuanced difference between brotherhoods and schools of Islamic law remained a mystery to be commented on occasionally over a Pimm's cup at the local club.

Local British attitudes toward Islam differed little from those of a period dime novel. British policy toward Islam was one of caution, principally to suppress Mahdism. Circulation of the Mahdi's writings was forbidden, his tomb was bombed, leading followers were imprisoned or kept under surveillance, and local Islamic brotherhoods were watched with suspicion. A Board of Ulema was created, its membership drawn from Islamic officials favorably viewed by the British for their loyalty. As such, it had no popular following, although it was asked to review all government proposals affecting Islam. Christian missionaries were excluded from the North by the British but were encouraged to settle in the South. Government money went toward the construction of mosques and support of the hajj. It was at this time that several important families, such as the Mirghanis, ingratiated themselves with the British.[13] Sayyid 'Ali al-Mirghani would emerge as a rival to Sayyid 'Abd al-Rahman, the Mahdi's son. The Mirghanis led the important Khatmiyyah *tariqa*; the Mahdi's followers joined the Ansar, the single largest political-religious group in Sudan. Although the two groups were rivals for decades, both shadow-boxed within the parameters available to them without ever challenging British rule.[14]

The Introduction of Mohammedan Law

In 1915 the British issued The Mohammedan Law Courts Ordinance and Procedure Regulations, drawn largely on previous colonial experience in India, as well as experience with the Sharia, which heavily influenced the Sudan Penal Code and its accompanying Code of Criminal Procedure.[15] It created a hierarchy of local Muslim courts supervised by the grand *qadi* at Khartoum.

In contrast, different policies were adopted in the South. Christian missionaries were urged to operate there, and a Muslim presence and the use of Arabic were discouraged; English-language education was encouraged; and northern troops were removed from local garrisons, which were staffed by southerners. What later was called a "southern policy," with major consequences for Sudan's history, thus began as a piecemeal, gerrymandered effort based on the attitudes and resources of local administrators rather than on any grand design.[16]

Two World Wars and the Rise of Nationalism: "Unity of the Nile Valley" versus "Sudan for the Sudanese"

Although Sudan had no direct role in World War I, it was still a time of galvanic change for the country. The first indications of a Sudanese national consciousness appeared at this time, the number of British officials was reduced, and the Ottoman Empire sided with the Central Powers. The local British response was to drop its hostility toward the *tariqas* and the Ansar. The Mahdi's son, Sayyid 'Abd al-Rahman, was freed. Reversing the departed Slatin's earlier, cautious policy, the British now toured 'Abd al-Rahman about the countryside, promoting him as a government loyalist. The trips achieved their immediate purpose but also created support for the Mahdi's son as a political personality in his own right, a force to be reckoned with at a later date.[17]

When in 1920 anonymous anti-British circulars began to appear in the streets of Khartoum, they were traced to the League of Sudan Union, and in 1922 a Dinka ex-officer was jailed for submitting an article calling for "self-determination for the Sudanese" to a local newspaper. The White Flag League, drawn from the ranks of government employees, supported the "unity of the Nile Valley." (The countervailing position was "Sudan for the Sudanese," the choice being closer ties with Egypt or Sudanese nationalism.) Later, as the educated class became more numerous, literary societies and short-lived newspapers of limited circulation sprung up, as they did in British-controlled Ireland. Such gestures and organizations had limited backers but represented the first stirrings of Sudanese nationalism, followed in 1924 by a crisis that ignited Sudanese anger against foreigners.

In that year Sudanese troops, caught between their sworn loyalty to an Egyptian king and the immediate command of a British officer to force the Egyptian troops from Khartoum North, refused the officer's order and were fired upon by the British. Retreating to the supposed shelter of a military hospital, all were killed in a British artillery attack.[18] The event became a benchmark in the collective consciousness of Sudanese, who were seeking to run a country of their own.

Meanwhile, the postwar British response to governing Sudan was to adopt a form of Indirect Rule, modeled on its Nigerian and Indian experiences. Necessitated by reduced numbers of available colonial administrators and resources, such a government would be staffed by supposedly loyal indigenous elites, educated for service in the administration and given limited powers. But the genie was out of the bottle, and whereas a smattering of loyalists emerged, so did a class of moderate nationalists and extremists. The positions taken by these latter two groups would affect the tenor of Sudanese political-religious history in the years ahead.

World War II and Emerging Nationalism

During World War II the Sudanese were actively engaged in conflict. The Italians were defeated in Eritrea, and the prospect of German dominance of the Nile Valley was removed with Rommel's defeat at El Alamein in November 1942. Once more, British administrative ranks were depleted and resources diminished, allowing heightened possibilities for Sudanese political activity. By the mid-1940s, the Ashigga Party emerged under Isma'il al-Azhari, formerly secretary-general of the thousand-member Graduates' General Congress, member of a long-standing family of reli-

gious leaders, and a mathematics graduate of American University of Be-
ruit. The party's pro-Egyptian stance was attractive to 'Ali al-Mirghani,
whose family had deep-rooted Egyptian ties. Meanwhile, his perennial
rival, Sayyid 'Abd al-Rahman, created the Umma ("nation") Party, favoring complete independence, which was to be gradually negotiated with
the British. With the Egyptian revolution of 1952, demands for Sudanese
self-determination quickened, resulting in independence on January 1,
1956.[19]

Seen in retrospect, the organizations that promoted nationalism in the
Sudan were made up primarily of long-established professional people,
such as members of the Graduates' General Congress. Such groups continued to exert influence, especially religious influence, after the British
had left. There was no experienced, smoothly running governmental superstructure to turn over the keys to at independence, and without secular
political parties, religiously based organizations became politically engaged
in a unique way. Voll remarks, "The distinction between state and society,
or between central state structures and societal institutions, is one of the
most important features of the relationship between Islam and the 'modern nation-state' in Sudan in the 20th century."[20]

New Times: Civilian Parliamentary and
Military Dictatorial Governments

Nothing went smoothly in subsequent Sudanese political life. In roughly
a half-century, independent Sudan oscillated between three parliamentary
governments, 1953–1958, 1965–1969, and 1986–1989, covering slightly
more than a decade, and three military dictatorships, 1958–1964, 1969–
1985, and 1989 on, extending over 40 years.[21] In each government, Islamic issues were a major determinant of public policy, as demonstrated
in the formation of political parties, the efforts to promulgate the Islamic
Constitution in 1968, the rise of Hasan al-Turabi as a religious-political
figure, the execution of the well-respected reformer Mahmud Muhammad
Taha in 1985, the 1983 introduction of the September Sharia laws, and
the coming to power in 1989 of the Islamic National Front as Sudan's
dominant political party. At every step the process was fraught with domestic and international controversy, including conflicts with neighboring
states and the West; a draining civil war; and an unending controversy
between rigid Islamists, whose goal was to turn Sudan into a religious
state, and more tolerant secularists, who promoted the separation of

church and state.[22] The summary of recent Sudanese history that follows highlights only significant attempts to build an Islamic state and their attendant problems.

The Islamic Constitution of 1968

A crucial event in modern Sudanese history was the Islamic Constitution of 1968. By then the country had experienced unsuccessful parliamentary and military regimes and sought a constitutional government that would provide stability and continuity in government. When a technical drafting committee convened in 1967, it considered three options—a fully Islamic constitution, with the Sharia as its foundation; a modified Islamic constitution; or a constitution in which religion and state were distinctly separate. The second option, a modified Islamic Constitution, was adopted by the Parliament. The constitution was a sectarian document. Chapter One declared that it was "derived from the principles and spirit of Islam," that "Islam is the official religion of the state, and Arabic its official language." Chapter Four established the Sharia as "the primary source of legislation," called for the repeal or amendment of all laws that contravened it, and said, "The state shall endeavor to spread religious (i.e., Islamic consciousness) among citizens and strive to purge society from atheism and all forms of moral corruption and lack of ethics."

Other articles granted free speech and free association, but always with the door-closing provision that no illegal change or political organization whose aims contradict the conditions established in the constitution could exist.[23] Influenced by al-Turabi, the drafters pushed for a document based on the premise that the Islamic religion and state were one, a solution satisfactory to its proponents but utterly unworkable in a modern pluralistic state. Some of its unanswered questions included the following: What was the place of non-Muslims in such a legal scheme? Would the new Sudanese political system be a theocracy or a democracy? What would the abolishing of ribba (interest) do to the country's commercial life? How compatible was the Sharia with a multireligious, multicultural society? What would prevent its Islamic proponents from abusing their power? As such questions suggest, the constitution, far from attracting widespread public confidence, became a source of anxiety, especially among southerners and opposition politicians.

The September (1983) Sharia Laws

Another military coup shelved the constitutional question, with all its implications for Sudanese life. Colonel Jaafar Muhammad al-Nimeiri, at the head of a group of young army officers, seized power on May 25, 1969. Al-Nimeiri ran the country for the next 16 years, during which the civil war between the North and South grew, Sudan's economy declined, inflation soared, foreign debt increased, and political life atrophied. Gradually al-Nimeiri abandoned his secular position for a pro-Islamic one; the officer (who promoted himself to the rank of major general) then declared that he was an imam.[24] Faced with a political and legal quagmire, on September 8, 1983, he promulgated a new penal code for the country based largely on the Sharia and incorporating its penal sanctions, including the punishment for crimes of theft, adultery, the consumption of alcohol, murder, and false accusations. Amputations, lashings, and executions were among the prescribed punishments. Moreover, the September decrees incorporated provisions of a 1973 state security act that further tightened restrictions of free speech and free assembly.[25]

The new laws solved nothing. They were followed by a strike of the country's once-respected judiciary; caused panic in the South;[26] brought the opprobrium of the international community once more; and left al-Nimeiri, by now the self-declared "imam of the whole Sudan," the ally of strident Islamists. From his power base he repealed 123 out of 225 articles of the country's earlier constitution that he found objectionable, reduced the legislature to a consultative body, and made himself a president for life with the title "leader of the faithful and shepherd of the Sudanese nation."[27]

As part of the regime's crackdown on potential critics, a respected 76-year-old scholar-reformer, Mahmud Muhammad Taha, was executed in January 1985. Trained as an engineer, Taha was a mystic and a theologian, popular with university students. He had been arrested by the British and jailed before independence for causing "disturbances." His advocacy of human rights and women's rights brought him in confrontation with the country's theocratic rulers. Taha argued that, although the Sharia was perfect, it required constant interpretation in different times and circumstances. The Islamic reformist was accused of apostasy for holding such views. He was tried by three respected judges, and his corpse was dangled by a helicopter circling over Khartoum for much of a day. Taha's death sent shock waves throughout the country, partly causing the Intifada uprising of students in March–April 1985.[28]

The Beleaguered State: The Coming to Power (1989) of the Islamic National Front

The twentieth century's final years in the Sudan were dominated by yet another authoritarian government that faced a daunting set of challenges, including a shattered economy; venality; and a demoralized public sector whose members' salaries had been shrunk by hyperinflation, drought, poverty, urban drift, illiteracy, and malnutrition. In addition, Sudan's civil war would claim an estimated 2 million people; possibly another 3 million were displaced by the war, and $1 million a day was consumed by military expenses. The 1989 coup led by Omar Hassan al-Bashir was greeted by a measure of relief both inside and outside the country. The population was disillusioned with the indecisiveness and incompetence of Sadiq al-Mahdi's civilian government. For those sympathetic to the aspirations of a government ruled by Islamic principles, it seemed a heaven-sent opportunity to show the world, as well as the war-weary population of Sudan, the virtues of basing the state's law and politics on Islam.

The sectarian nature of the Muslim community and its political organizations has been a formative aspect of Sudanese politics. Until the military-NIF (National Islamic Front) coup in 1989, competition within ruling coalitions occupied the creative energies of civilian governments, to the detriment of national leadership and development. With multiple sectarian parties competing for national power, no one party was able to gain more than 42% of the vote. To form a national government, winning parties had to share power with roughly equal partners and their competing agendas. Coalition governments proved woefully unstable, with members eager to unseat their partners from the beginning. With the country beset by paralysis and confusion, popular government support evaporated.

Meanwhile, the new government soon perceived itself to be surrounded by enemies. Within a year, it had alienated virtually all neighboring states, as well as the United States, which had supported Khartoum through many vicissitudes. As the NIF emerged as a driving force behind domestic and foreign policy, outside observers feared that the only African country under Islamist rule would spread the germ of political Islam to its African and Arab neighbors. Longtime supporters in Saudi Arabia and Kuwait were alienated by Sudan's declaration of support for Iraq in the Gulf war, its announcement of a 1990 alliance with Libya (though it never got off the ground), and Khartoum's courtship of Iran, which in fact brought it only meager assistance.

Western criticism of human rights abuses, the authoritarian methods of the military government, and its toleration, if not active support, of terrorist organizations[29] prompted warnings of retaliation. The Sudanese leadership was well aware that hostile actions by the United States could easily destroy the country's fragile economy. This awareness of vulnerability—and the August 20, 1998, U.S. missile strike against a suspected chemical weapons–producing site in Khartoum, the El Shifa pharmaceutical plant—opened the way for hard-line Islamists to resist practical measures for change demanded by the West. At each step along this downward spiral, high Sudanese government officials reiterated the charge that the West harbors an enduring enmity toward Islam and is not motivated by a concern for human rights, democracy, or terrorism.

Meanwhile, increasing international opprobrium was aimed at the Sudan, which was called a pariah state and a harbor for terrorists, including Osama bin Laden. "Islam is the Solution" proclaimed Revolution of National Salvation soldier-politicians, who came to power in a June 30, 1989, coup, but addressing Sudan's multiple challenges was another matter.

Sudan's government was faced with a thorny problem, which it grasped with both hands. It sought to both retain the Sharia and present a federal-type power-sharing arrangement to attract southerners. But the NIF's proposed charter had too many escape valves; it was never clear which powers would be retained by the central government, and buried in the charter was an explosive provision that allowed the government to suspend laws during a national emergency, which could be declared at any time. Negotiations raised southern fears about the Sharia once again, plus additional objections that the proposed document contravened provisions of the Universal Declaration of Human Rights. It proved to be a stumbling block rather than an instrument of national unity.[30]

In 1993 General Umar Hasan al-Bashir, having gradually consolidated his power base, dissolved the 15-member Revolutionary Command Council for National salvation and declared himself president. The NIF, led by Hasan al-Turabi, at that time a close ally of Bashir, was also in the ascendancy. Officer ranks of the army and university faculty were purged, women were dismissed from positions as government clerks and teachers, and NIF members were given most cabinet positions.

Efforts to portray the civil war as a jihad did nothing to bring it toward resolution. A $13 billion debt assumed in the 1989 takeover, rioting over inflation, and the introduction of new currencies that did nothing to help the economy were only some of the problems al-Bashir and his allies faced. Meanwhile, the Sudan continued to lose international allies, in part for its siding with Sadam Hussain's Iraq, and charges of torture, genocide, extrajudicial detentions, and killings were rife. [31]

What becomes evident in sorting out the arduous trail of contemporary Sudanese Islamic politics is that its religiously oriented proponents descended early on into the political maelstrom, which of necessity involved compromise and conflict—frustrating purists and pragmatists alike—and produced meager results. Sidahmed has written, "In its eagerness to lay its hands on power, the Sudanese Islamist movement seems to have endorsed and legitimized the game of politics with all its cynicism and shameless pursuit of partisan interests at the expense of religious morality and principles."[32]

Furthering Islam: War with the South

Parenthetically, the Islamist view that shaped much of Khartoum's defensiveness toward the rest of the world also shaped its policies toward the South, which has been at war with the North much of the time since 1955, the year before independence. The war has demonstrated some of the fundamental problems arising out of Sudan's fragmented political plight during the past half-century. The close link between religion and nationalist political agendas has meant that accommodation is difficult to achieve, with leadership on both sides focusing on issues of power rather than compromise. Negotiations during the 1990s, for example, have shown that neither side was willing to arrive at a peace accord unless the other side totally capitulated. The South's negotiating possibilities were further weakened by numerous competing ethnic and religious divisions, often within the same groups.

The demands of Sudanese People's Liberation Army (SPLA) leader John Garang centered on establishing a secular government and the removal of sectarian political parties from the national scene. For his faction, Numayri's September Laws symbolized northern injustice and the South's historically inferior status.[33]

Both civilian and military regimes in the North have resisted proposals for a federal state and have insisted on centralized political control, Islam as the state religion, and Arabic as Sudan's official language. Government officials see Islamization of the South as a duty. As a result, the September Laws' extreme interpretation of Sharia, which provided a harsh model of a modern political state, were modified, although never enough to meet southern demands.[34]

The war's seesaw nature, with its annual victory rituals, has also contributed to the Sudanese regime's paranoia about the outside world—

Western governments, the United Nations (UN), and nongovernmental organizations (NGOs) that have operated freely in the South and actively supported the SPLA against Khartoum.[35] A typical official response to intervention from abroad has been the statement that the regime "will never accept outside political pressures designed to make Sudan get down on its knees."[36] But renewed demands for cooperation with the West in the post–September 11, 2001, period and the appointment of a special American envoy to the Sudan resulted in a more optimistic framework in international relations.

Signs of Change?

Sudan's Islamic government continues to control the political arena and monopolize power through its extensive security forces, although multiple sources estimate that it no longer has the support of the large majority of the population. A new constitution, endorsed by referendum and signed into law by al-Bashir in June 1998, may represent a first step toward formally liberalizing the regime. The NIF junta is officially committed to democratization, although not Western-style liberal democratization, which it believes is "too divisive and dysfunctional" for a country like Sudan. The rulers prefer a form of citizen committee rule, which would function by the Islamic concept of *shura* (consultation). In response to Western demands for democratization, the government claims that it is gradually establishing democracy from the grassroots up.

In the late 1990s, the NIF has moved toward policies of inclusion, including old sectarian enemies, and is ignoring Muslim and non-Muslim distinctions in seeking political allies. There have been meetings between al-Turabi and Umma Party leaders. In November 1999, the head of state, al-Bashir, signed an agreement with the former prime minister, Sadiq al-Mahdi, who had been living in exile abroad. Earlier in the year, al-Bashir invited the former president, Jaafar al-Numayri, to return home from exile in Egypt. The leadership of the SPLA-United, a breakaway group from the SPLA, and other rebel groups made their peace with Khartoum in 1998 and were given prominent positions in the government.

The political divisions fostered by sectarian parties since independence give Sudan a tradition of party politics and some experience of the power of Sharia in a multiparty government. By March 1999, 38 political parties were licensed, their membership reflecting the complexity of politics in the Sudan. They include the following:

- The Ruling National Congress Party, now headed by al-Bashir, which is competing with other parties in sectors—such as the universities, intellectuals, women, and youths—where it formerly could count on support
- The Muslim Brothers' Party, calling for moral redemption through Islamic law, which represents Islamist conservatives who are convinced the government is not sufficiently Muslim
- A breakaway Democratic Unionist Party (DUP), headed by former DUP officials
- The Sudanese Central Movement, a centrist party along lines of the former DUP, which is appealing to politically moderate Muslims
- The mainstream Umma Party, the political party led by former prime minister Sadiq al-Mahdi, which has criticized the government for allowing the return of Numayri and has joined forces with former head of state Ahmad al-Mirghani's DUP leadership in exile to form the National Democratic Alliance (NDA), representing conservative Islam-based political orientation and reflecting mainstream northern viewpoints
- A Umma Party faction
- The People's Working Forces Alliance, the party of Numayri's followers
- The United Democratic Salvation Front (UDSF) under Riek Machar, which has solid backing in the South among most of the southern factions and has signed the 1997 Khartoum Peace Agreement

According to a former U.S. ambassador to Khartoum, Donald Petterson, there are increasingly differences of opinion within the ruling establishment over the future direction of government policies.[37] European observers familiar with the situation in Khartoum believe that a "pragmatic engagement with the outside world" and concern about the government's image abroad[38] is emerging and that there is a new focus on solving Sudan's internal problems rather than spreading an Islamist revolution throughout the Muslim world. Thus, Petterson writes that Khartoum urged Osama bin Laden, once a favored wealthy resident and commercial presence, to move to Afghanistan after 1996 when he had become a clear embarrassment to the government's efforts to soften its image as a state sponsor of terrorism.[39]

Sudan's relations with the United States took a new turn following the September 11, 2001, terrorist attacks in New York and Washington.

The Sudanese government condemned the attacks, but also the American bombing of Afghanistan. It rounded up some 30 foreign extremist suspects residing in Sudan, including al Qaida network members, and cooperated in tracing bank records, but it also continued its bombing attacks on the South, disrupting the distribution of relief supplies by international agencies.

In an effort to improve relations, it also disclosed a 1996 offer to arrest Osama bin Laden, then living in Khartoum and operating a successful construction business. The plan, the work of American and Sudanese intelligence operatives, was to arrest bin Laden and turn him over to the Saudis, who presumably would dispose of him quickly. However, the Saudis declined to participate in the plan, probably because of bin Laden's close family and financial ties with the Saudi royal family. Presumably at American insistence, bin Laden was then expelled from Sudan on May 18, 1996, taking his staff and money with him by private plane to Afghanistan. Sudanese officials pointed out that had he remained in Khartoum, it would have been easy to track his moves and transactions, which was not the case in Afghanistan. As a result of Sudan's increased cooperation, the Bush administration asked the UN Security Council to lift sanctions against Sudan that had been in force for 5 years. A special envoy, former Senator John Danforth, was appointed to help improve relations and broker a North-South accord.[40]

The government has also achieved modest success in mending fences with immediate neighbors. Both Eritrea and Ethiopia, distracted by their own quarrels, have virtually ended overt support for the southern rebels, and relations with the governments of Egypt, Libya, and Algeria have improved as hostility in the wake of the 1995 Mubarak assassination attempt has subsided.

Khartoum also appears to be trying yet again to develop a workable formula for internal peace, suggesting compromise with all faction leaders in the South with promises of self-determination and the choice by referendum of full independence. In the words of the SPLA-United leader, Riek Machar, "The government is Islamist. But . . . they know Islam is not threatened by the South [and that] war isn't the way to go about spreading Islam."[41] There is a growing perception in both North and South that Sudan does not fit the profile of the Arab club of North Africa and the Middle East. A number of observers believe that the Sudanese increasingly regard ties between the North and South within Sudan as more important to their economic well-being than relations with other African countries.

The Rise and Fall of Hasan al-Turabi as a Religious-Political Figure

No figure in modern Sudanese Islamic history is more important or more controversial than Hasan al-Turabi. Married into the distinguished al-Mahdi family, he was educated in Great Britain and at the Sorbonne and was the first Sudanese to receive a doctorate in philosophy. The son of an Islamic judge, al-Turabi became dean of Khartoum University's Law School until 1965 and was elected to Parliament. He was attorney general, 1979–1983, and later held the posts of minister of justice, minister of foreign affairs, and deputy prime minister.[42]

A prolific writer and scholar, he gained an international reputation as an Islamic theorist and was sought after as a featured speaker at international think-tank conferences on Islam and modernization. But at home, al-Turabi's name is associated with most repressive measures of the governments he helped lead. He began public life as a member of the fundamentalist Muslim Brotherhood at the University of Khartoum, and for al-Turabi politics and religion were always inextricable. From the Muslim Brotherhood he moved to the Islamic Charter Front, as the brotherhood reconstituted itself, and then the National Islamic Front, which was formed after the 1985 coup and which became the main voice of the coup regime. His was the intellectual voice behind the introduction of the Sharia as the basis of Sudanese law.

Yossef Bodansky links al Turabi to support of numerous terrorist groups, generally ideologically influenced by Iran and financially backed by Osama bin Laden, who was resident in Sudan from 1991 to 1996. They include a planning role in the June 26, 1995, assassination attempt on Egypt's President Mubarak, then visiting Addis Ababa, Ethiopia, and with the organizers of the August 7, 1998, terrorist attacks on American embassies in Nairobi, Kenya, and Dar-es-Salaam, Tanzania.[43]

Though small of stature, al-Turabi was not lacking in ego. Of Egypt's President Mubarkek he said, "I found the man to be very far below my level of thinking and my views, and too stupid to understand my pronouncements."[44] In the interviews al-Turabi gave to journalists and scholars, listeners were bombarded with theology, jurisprudence, and rhetoric, and since the speaker rarely stopped talking, pinning him down was impossible. To some, al-Turabi initially appeared as a progressive. His 1973 pamphlet, "The Woman in Islamic Teachings," was far ahead of its time, arguing that a woman had a duty to defy her family in fulfillment of her religious obligations, that the Koran ensured the protection of women against men, and that women should be considered independently from males in religious discourse.[45] Yet thousands of women have been dismissed from their government jobs, female genital mutilation remains widespread, and few women hold political positions of any importance.

"The State Repenting to Islam": Al-Turabi

Al-Turabi was often painted as an Islamic pragmatist who sponsored a brand of Islamic economics and allowed the presence of popular Islam and sectarianism. Undergirding his basic viewpoint was the idea of "the state repenting to Islam" and all laws and regulations leading to the Sharia.[46] Islamic renewal must take into consideration that the jurisprudence established by early generations of believers is incomplete, he argued, especially when it confronts public administration and economics.[47] Nevertheless, Islam can address such issues; this occurs by first a political and then a legal revolution, and the former can be realized only by the conversion of individual members of society to Islam's true path. First the individual, then the state. In an intermediary stage, a group of converted believers should form and propagate their faith by any available method, such as coups and revolutions. And they should lay out blueprints for what constitutes an Islamic political polity, the cornerstone of which is Sharia. "Over and over again al-Turabi implores his audiences to believe that Islamic society is not static, but that the only way to go anywhere is to go there [to the most familiar version of Sharia] first,"[48] Simone observes. Such an intellectual construct provides, inter alia, a lucid ideological justification for the groups from which their sponsor has operated for half a century. It is not that al-Turabi was an unreconstructed traditionalist; in fact, he has moved each organization he has been a member of in modern directions—but only to a point, and never to a place where they could contest his control.[49]

Boasting that Sudan's new oil money will be used to buy weapons to pursue the war against the South[50]—rather than for confidence-building measures or assistance to the poverty-stricken populations of both North and South—al-Turabi has been an important influence in hardening Islamist attitudes. In 1993, the U.S. Embassy called him the "preeminent" force in the NIF government. Unremittingly hostile to U.S. power, al-Turabi said that America was contaminating the world as "a racist, godless society . . . with no moral compass and a philosophy of 'whatever works goes.' "[51] Although he has seen himself at the center of a new Islamic revival that would sweep away the old order in Muslim countries throughout the world, his position has been fading since the 1996 parliamentary election and the commensurate increase in al-Bashir's power. He is not out of the picture yet, however. Younger NIF leaders, such as Ali Osman Taha and Ghazi Salah Eddin, respect him as an intellectual mentor from the past, but they have thrown their lot enthusiastically with Bashir and have established their own independent positions.[52] Al-Turabi has written the book on Islamist ideology in Sudan. Although there are moderates in the government willing to take practical steps to meet Western demands, they do not control the government. Hard-line Islamists, strengthened by evidence of Western hostility—and the seeming reluctance of Garang to end the civil war—are still able to doggedly resist change.

Al-Turabi was not without enemies. His manner could irritate friends and opponents alike, and he spent more than seven years in prison, most recently during the term of his close ally, President Omar Hassan al-Bashir. Al-Turabi was jailed on February 22, 2001, after his party, now the Popular National Congress Party, met unannounced with representatives of the Sudanese People's Liberation Army in Geneva and signed a joint accord calling for peaceful resistance to the government. Response from the president was swift; al-Turabi and at least 150 of his followers were jailed.[53] Al-Turabi's family complained that formal charges were never presented against him, a due process complaint often raised against the former jurist when he was in power. Next Bashir played a Kafkaesque cat-and-mouse game with his former ally. Al-Turabi and his associates were kept in detention; then charges were dropped against the others, and finally against al-Turabi on October 1, 2001, but he was still kept under house arrest in a government building and allowed visits only once a week from family members.[54] The once-leading figure in Sudanic political and religious life was stripped of his influence and dignity.

The Discrepancy between Theory and Practice in al-Turabi's Life and Politics

There is a discrepancy in al-Turabi's thought, an ambiguity between what the projected state might be and how it could be realized. Coups posed no moral problem for al-Turabi (the NIF came to power in such a manner, with no mandate other than its own). Popular participation in government has no moral grounding in his arguments, as Sudan is not a democracy. Despite external trappings, such as relative freedom in dress codes and an occasionally free press, Sudan remains one of Africa's most repressive societies, buttressed by legions of state security agents and their dreaded "ghost house" interrogation centers.

Tracking al-Turabi's views leads to the conclusion that he shaped them to fit his audiences, seeking to gain support in Sudan's turbulent political setting, but their roots remain in the rigid Islamism of his early years. By spending so much time in the political sphere, al-Turabi the opportunist emerged as a figure closer in viewpoint to Machiavelli, a political theorist of expediency, than as a mystic or saint. And despite the intensity of his religious pronouncements on Sharia questions, his voice was not found among those who opposed Sudan's frequent military takeovers or the corrupt practices of its agents, who inhabit the massive homes of recent vintage in Khartoum's suburbs. Above all, he was the long-time intellectual apologist for a religiously constructed state system that has left Sudan a shambles.

Overview and Conclusion: A Subtly Shifting Landscape

In the late 1990s, the Sudanese government leadership drawn from the NIF has moved toward the politics of inclusion. The Islamists have assembled an electoral commission and a parliamentary assembly, and they have offered a referendum on self-determination to the South. The new Constitution assigns major offices to civilians rather than to the military and allows a gradual evolution toward democratization of the government's authoritarian structure. These moves continue to be framed within the dimensions of Islamic law and envisage the use of *shura* (consensus) rather than majority rule in the decision-making process.

As a result of these changes and their acceptance by populations in the North and South, the fundamental divide within the country no longer cuts theologically between Muslim and non-Muslim or geographically between northern and southern regions. The fault lines lie among the al-Bashir regime, with its strong NIF component; Garang and the Southerners; and Sadiq al-Mahdi, together with the leaders of the sectarian parties of the North—in other words, among proponents of an Islamic, or a secular, nonreligious state.

Islamic government is here to stay in Sudan. Al-Turabi's star may have set, and al-Bashir, considered the more pragmatic leader, may have emerged as the predominant voice in the government. Al-Bashir remains adamant on the centrality of Islam's political role and rejects any proposal to remove the religious dimension from government, maintaining that all three of the major northern parties are in fact focused on Islamization. He writes that "the centerpiece of the program of the al-Umma party of al-Mahdi is the Islamic awakening; and that of the Democratic Unionist Party, the Islamic Republic, and the agenda of the Islamic National Front promotes the implementation of a Sharia-based legal system. All of them are identical, only they have different leaders." Al-Bashir claims to offer a more broadly representational government—not "a coalition government where each party would have its own agenda [but] a harmonious administration committed to a single program."[55] But beneath his conciliatory rhetoric, his goals continue to be retention of power, the Islamization of Sudan, aid to radical Muslim causes abroad, and encouragement of political Islam worldwide.

To summarize: the Islamic community in the Sudan is not and never has been a monolithic structure religiously, politically, or socially. It comprises:

- The two major brotherhoods: the Khatmiyyah, based in northern and eastern districts of Sudan and led by the Mirghani family, influential behind-the-scenes power brokers, and the Mahdi family, members of the Sammaniyya brotherhood, based in central and western Sudan, active since its beginnings under the Mahdi in the nineteenth century. They support an Islamist political state but would modify the harsh form of Sharia imposed by President Numayri in the 1983 September laws.
- Minor Sufi brotherhoods[56] with considerable local power but little national influence. It was from these groups that President Numayri sought support for passage of his September Laws in 1983.[57]
- The newer Muslim Brotherhood, which has appealed to an emerging intellectual class through its NIF party platform. (The Muslim Brotherhood, originating as a student organization in the 1940s, was the ground from which the traditionalist intellectual al-Turabi operated.) The NIF advocates an antisectarian and antisecular program that calls for replacement of the mainstream northern conservative, sectarian politics by redemptive Islamist reforms and imposition of the Sharia as the national code of law.
- A growing number of the educated elite, such as Prime Minister Ismail al-Azhari, the leader of Sudan's first democratic government. This group opposes sectarianism and does not support brotherhood political parties, but it also advocates an Islamic republic with laws based on Islamic principles.

The Future of Sharia: Here to Stay

Political realities rather than religious fanaticism have kept Sudanese politicians from revising or removing the September Laws. Rather than confront this key issue of legal reform, they shroud it in rhetoric. The major parties in the north find that there are good, practical, political reasons for adopting visibly Islamic policies. The majority of the northern population, and therefore of the Sudan, includes people with a modern lifestyle experience, who identify themselves as profoundly Muslim. Opposition to Islamization in northern Sudan focuses on Numayri's particularly harsh application of Sharia, not on the essential value of Islamic law for the North. For this reason, Sadiq al-Mahdi has consistently argued that the September Laws in their present form are not truly Islamic. What Numayri accomplished, in the view of mainstream northern Muslims, was to show that Islamic law could be imposed on a national basis. If the wishes of the Sudanese majority are to be followed, change will have to come by making the law more Islamic, not less, that is, by modifying the application of criminal punishments (*hudud*) and allowing non-Muslims their separate legal institutions.

Proponents of democratization will need to account for the enduring commitment of Sudan's northern population to the Islamic revival. It seems likely that if given a choice between a secular form of government and one based on Islamic law, the population would chose the latter, however much they dislike its harsh application. Thus, insistence on a secular Sudan by a segment of southern leadership is probably politically impractical—unless its proponents prefer to continue the present stalemate. The experience of recent years indicates that changing the majority's preference for some form of Islamic rule is unlikely for the foreseeable future. Sudanese Muslims will see efforts by the West to hasten such a process, however well meaning, as part of an ongoing crusade against Islam, sharpening the paranoia of a beleaguered society. At the same time, the inescapable conclusion is that the chasm between state and society looms large in Sudan, and Islam, for whatever its religious attraction, "continues to be a factor of disunity"[58] in national life.

The authoritarian Islamic government of Sudan has begun to make cautious moves toward a more open, more inclusive political system. The sharp divisions that have characterized the postindependence period— between the North and the South and between Muslims and non-Muslims—have begun to blur, but politics in Sudan remains a balancing act between extremes.[59] Many northern politicians, under the guise of espousing Islamic purity, have used religion to consolidate their own political power, pointedly ignoring what many other countries have discovered: that a federalist state can accommodate pluralistic viewpoints. The government is now seeking ways to compromise with southern rebel factions that continue to be unreconciled to the establishment of an Islamic government in Khartoum. Although the infamous September Laws—the symbol of Sudan's destructive religious divisions—remain on the books, most northerners support the Islamic state but reject Numayri's draconian formula and favor moderate, consensus-based political institutions that will work. However, a secular alternative has little or no appeal for them, and demands for the removal of Islam from Sudanese politics are unlikely to produce positive negotiating results.

Analyzing the history of Islam in modern Sudan is like considering a computer software program that has gone awry. If the *traditionalist-Sharia* button is pressed, it is neutralized by the *secular constitutionalist* one. *North* and *South* block each other, and *parliamentary democracy* is checked by *military dictatorship*. When *nation-state* is highlighted, it is blocked by war, famine, disease, pestilence, drought, and illiteracy. And if the country is positioned in the Arab world, some other Arab states consider it a quarrelsome, backward cousin; nor does it fit easily into Africa either. A vibrant, energetic people remains frustrated at every turn by its own history and religion-based politics.[60]

Islam in Senegal

Maintaining a Delicate Balance

Senegal's Muslim community, which has been an epicenter of West African politics and Islam in the past, is at the threshold of major institutional changes as the postcolonial era ends and a new generation of Senegalese political and religious leadership emerges. A shift in the balance of power is taking place among the Sufi brotherhoods (*tariqa*),[1] which virtually account for Senegal's population, and this in turn is undermining the cooperative religious tolerance that various governments have assiduously promoted. The country's Muslim leaders are aging. Generational tensions trouble Muslim institutions, and succession to their leadership and control remains uncertain. Youthful delinquency, growing out of rapid urbanization and unemployment, becomes increasingly difficult for Muslim leaders to control and threatens the fabric of society. As the Senegalese economy deteriorates, traditional agricultural practices that have enriched a segment of the Muslim community are now detrimental to the whole country's well-being. Muslim commercial entities are moving out from Senegal's shaky economic platform to form worldwide commercial networks with strong U.S. and European components. They will probably affect the pace of political and social change at home.

In the near term, the traditional symbiotic relationship between mosque and secular state is likely to continue as government officials and religious leaders act together to coopt and contain extremist Islamist tendencies and urban disorder. Within the next decade, however, a vigorously expanding Mouride brotherhood is likely to overwhelm its Muslim rivals and challenge the central government's authority. Furthermore, youthful Muslim activists with a reformist, utopian program, promising a more equal distribution of wealth and better living standards, will challenge the brotherhoods' present staid, inward-looking leadership. Either course of events could upend Senegal's conservative secular and religious establishments and threaten the fragile stability of one of the West's most dependable African allies.

Relations at the Knife-Edge: French Policies and Expansive Islam in the Senegambia, Nineteenth–Twentieth Centuries

"If one should throw . . . a knife to a person that is drowning he is sure to grasp it although it will cut his hands and . . . would not save him" (from the report of a Messenger to Chief Beram Ceesay, August 18, 1880, describing the likelihood that the Muslim chief would take aid from the French).[2]

Senegambia was a society in the throes of violent change by the nineteenth century. An expansive Muslim community and the stresses induced into traditional societies by the slave trade had left the region's traditional states ripe for revolution, and the new Islamic presence provided both an affirming identity for people and a way of opposing the encroachments of European rule.[3]

The French, British, and Portuguese had been trading in the region since the sixteenth century. France established trading centers at St. Louis and Albreda on the Senegal and Gambia Rivers, but despite the long-term European presence these settlements were isolated by hostility and fear. There was little understanding of the African communities around them. Incidents of violence were frequent, and the small numbers of Europeans were periodically expelled from their trading posts during the eighteenth century.

Meanwhile, Islam had peacefully worked its way into the region down trade routes from the north, as part of the intellectual baggage of Berber traders and travelers, until it reached the lower Senegal River. First merchants, then clerics—that was the pattern, although some merchants were also clerics who contributed to the expansion of Islam. The merchants moved along established routes and opened newer ones in less-frequented regions. Then came the clerics, often accompanying larger commercial caravans, sometimes staying with an individual chief or town as imam or teacher.[4] Such figures generally led simple lives of prayer; they do not appear to have mingled much in politics, and the brand of Islamic belief that emerged in the region became heavily interlarded with local practices, a distinctive feature of Islam in Senegal. Levtzion has concluded, "Islam in the area of present-day Senegal was always somewhat different from other parts of Bilad al-Sudan [Land of the Black People]; it resembled more the Sahara, from Morocco to the Senegal River, where the ocean's influence moderates the harsh desert conditions."[5]

At the beginning of the eleventh century, the first of the several waves of Muslim revival and reform exploded into the northern Senegambia from the Mauritanian desert sand just north of the Senegal River. The Almoravids were a Berber religious order founded in what is now Mauritania. They attacked the pagan empire of Ghana with a series of military hammer blows, Islamized Ghana's leadership, and drove the center of West African political power eastward. There, large states emerged that employed Islamic law and bureaucratic organization to create peaceful conditions along the desert's Sudanic borders. Some semblance of state organization was in place, and peaceful influence and control extended over wide areas. Civility in public discourse was a feature of society, and travelers could pass through the region without fear of robbers. Ibn Battuta, a world traveler like his near contemporary Marco Polo, toured the Mali empire in 1352–1353 and wrote that its rulers "are seldom unjust, and have a greater horror of injustice than other people. Their sultan shows no mercy to anyone who is guilty of the least act of it. There is complete security in their country. Neither traveler nor inhabitant in it has anything to fear from robbers or men of violence."[6]

Ruling elites, merchant classes, and town dwellers converted to Islam in the Sahel region and forest fringes, and the gradual conversion of the Senegambia continued through the seventeenth century, moving from urban areas into the countryside. Its agents were merchants, scholars, and clerics; religious specialists functioning as political, religious, and moral guides; judges; doctors; and diviners.

The emerging Muslim states in the region acted as intermediaries between desert and forest and between seekers and sources of wealth, including the rising Tekrur and Wolof kingdoms. Islam, however, was still a supplementary rather than a replacement religion with steps backward (Songhay), as well as forward. The point is important, for West African Islam has always maintained its distinctive characteristics, amalgamating Koranic belief with strongly held local traditions and gravitating around local figures, many of them drawn from the Sufi mystical tradition.[7]

By the fourteenth and fifteenth centuries, Muslim traders were moving south into the Upper Niger and Voltaic regions. By then, Islam had begun to offer services to a wider population—providing schools, hospitals, markets, law courts, the means to tap into trade networks, literacy, and an increasingly strong cultural identity. To the court leadership of these West African states, Islam provided legitimacy and power, an accessible system of governing, a framework of law, and a broader field of contact. But sources for this epoch are thin, and the Portuguese accounts of this period say little about Islam and less about the countryside. However, if the diffusion of religious belief followed patterns seen elsewhere, in the conservative countryside people still held to traditional beliefs; farmers, cattle herders, and fishermen remained aloof or made some accommodations, balancing traditional pagan practices with new Islamic teachings.

It was only from the seventeenth to the nineteenth centuries that Islam moved to the position of a minority culture coequal with other cultures and belief systems. Probably at this time Islam was a majority religion among the Tukulor and perhaps the Wolof.[8] Meanwhile, thousands of Muslim communities, many of them small and temporary, were established along trade routes and in commercial centers. References to wandering *mallams* and *sherifs* in the countryside appear, but by the nineteenth century, Islam as a quietistic force wore thin and an aggressive reform movement was experienced in parts of West Africa. As a result, the nineteenth century is known as the jihadist era. It was fed by memories in past glories in the age of empires; the spread of literacy and knowledge of wider Islamic movements; and opposition to corrupt, pagan societies and to the social and economic upheavals brought to West Africa by the slave trade. In many ways, the jihadist agenda was similar to the dissatisfactions voiced by today's Muslim activists. Islamist reformers rekindled a militant, revivalist tradition, not seen since the days of the Almoravids. They saw their task as a struggle for an ideal society based on a greater emphasis on the Koran and Hadith (traditions of the Prophet) as guides to the way in which a Muslim should live and a society should be governed.

The Sufis were important to the story then and to the African Muslim community now. Followers of a mystical, ecstatic dimension of Islam, they taught that through Sufi learning and practice, the individual can seek personal communion with God, usually under the guidance of a saintly master. Sufis have been notably willing to incorporate traditional practices, such as the wearing of charms and the use of local patterns of worship and music, into Islamic practice. In Africa, they have formed brotherhoods called *tariqas* (variously named Tijaniya, Qadiriya, Mouridiya, etc.), which traditionally wielded great political power. Cutting across social and family lines and providing stability and welcome to members, 2 centuries later Sufis retain the loyalty of the vast majority of African Muslims despite the higher profile of reformers.

The jihadists failed to create lasting states but opened the door for fundamental change, spreading Islam widely. And, in Nigeria, for example, theirs is a model held up by present-day reformers, although the original jihadists never prescribed a state structure once the old order was destroyed. (The word *jihad* is often misunderstood. In the nineteenth century, West Africa jihads were wars waged against nonbelievers, but such wars were fought most bitterly against Muslims considered lax in their practices. Violence was and is the last and least emphasized resort for those seeking reform and change. The "jihad of the word," in bringing about reform and conversion to Islam, usually suffices for all but the very few.)

The Colonial Encounter: A New Dynamic

Meanwhile, the French and British had been struggling to maintain their footing on the slippery slope of trade and military activity in the region.[9] For at least the first half of the nineteenth century, the French Senegalese settlements were somnolent, with only a minimal trading and administrative presence. Senegal had 30 governors in 33 years, some of whom never left Paris, and it was not until the arrival of Governor Louis Faidherbe in 1854 that French authority was established over the Senegal River Valley. There was trade in gum arabic, used in printing, and in groundnuts (peanuts), used in the making of soap. Inland the recalcitrant *marabouts* (revered teachers) were confronted with a superior military force.

Interactions between Africans and Europeans and the emerging European presence were demonstrated by the French clash with El Hajj Umar and also symbolized by the less well-known career of the Muslim leader and jihadist Maba Diakhou Ba (c. 1809–1867). The son of a *marabout*, Maba attended a Koranic school and eventually opened one of his own under a large tree that dominated the Ker Maba site, where he taught for several years as an increasingly respected scholar. He began preaching between the Saloum and Gambia Rivers, a region divided into small kingdoms governed by animist Mandinka rulers. Eventually, Maba met with the Muslim empire builder, El Hajj Umar; was initiated by him into a Sufi brotherhood; and was encouraged to wage holy war against lapsed Muslims and nonbelievers.[10]

Little is known of his personality, but a colony of other *marabouts* developed around Maba, and soon he became a military leader as well.

At this time, the pre-Islamic Senegambia states were torn by disputes between pastoralists and agriculturalists and merchants and their rulers, threatened by the arrival of British traders and the French military. After conquering the region, Maba imposed Islamic government on large areas previously untouched by Islam. He appointed Muslim judges to administer the Sharia and established schools throughout the region. However, Maba's desire to unify the whole of Senegambia soon clashed with the expanding French presence. First they collaborated with him, later they feared his power and expelled him for a while, and finally they killed him in battle in 1867.

Maba and other Muslim leaders hoped to establish states that for a while had seemed possibly to set the stage for a civil order not seen in the region since Mali and the medieval flowering of Islam. They were thwarted, however, by French suspicions that strong African states would make their commercial and imperial ambitions impossible. Ironically, it was during the subsequent colonial period that Islam really expanded in the region. Colonial administrators had few resources at their disposal and found the leadership of Muslim communities useful in keeping the peace and developing colonial economies. For Muslims, energy could now be turned from warfare to trade and to converting pagans with little opposition.

There was a Darwinian aspect to French policy. Muslims were held suspect but clearly a step above pagans, though below European Christians. Militant or fractious leaders were quickly removed. *Fiches de renseignement*—report cards—were kept on chiefs, grading each on their attitude toward France. Most proved malleable and cooperative with the French. Traditional chiefs' tasks included collecting taxes, finding workers for road gangs, and recruiting conscripts for the French army in World Wars I and II. Muslim chiefs were rewarded by the administration with recognition, trips to Mecca, and donations toward the construction of mosques. Many Muslims were suspicious of enrolling their immediate heirs in government or mission schools for fear of losing or contaminating them. Instead, they sent sons of lesser wives or slaves, and such persons in turn learned to read and write and assumed positions of power as clerks and interpreters in the emerging colonial government.

The story of France's encounter with Islam in Senegal has been variously told.[11] In broad outline, it is one of resistance followed by accommodation. France in the mid-nineteenth century was moving into a region that had experienced a number of jihads. What emerged was a relationship of mutual benefit between conquering power and conquered people.

The most evident characteristic of Islamic leaders in Senegal during the colonial era was their easy cooperation with the French. No coordinated opposition to the French presence ever emerged, as it did in Algeria, although some Islamic leaders withdrew spiritually and physically. But many Muslims, skilled traders and adroit negotiators, tried over decades to manipulate the French within the possibilities open to them. For example, the Mourides were viewed with suspicion by the French and at first opposed the French incursions, but by World War I they were encouraging people to support France against Germany. As a result of their loyalty, large tracts of land and trading concessions were granted to them. Some became known as *marabouts de l'arachide* (peanut *marabouts*), who spent as much time on secular commerce as they did on religious affairs. By 1914 groundnut production had reached 300,000 tons, and soon the numbers would double.[12]

If some Muslim groups consolidated power under the French, the European presence was not without destructive aspects as well. In the Sine-Saloum area of Senegal, the French occupation destroyed traditional states. Moreover the initial agricultural prosperity proved a mixed blessing. Senegal's economic and transportation infrastructure remained under French control, and with the eventual decline in market prices farmers went into debt. In addition, reliance on a single cash crop led to eventual economic and ecological disaster.

The Emergence of Islamic Brotherhoods: Mouridiya and Tijaniya

Two large Islamic brotherhoods emerged at this time as the central force of social cohesion in an otherwise volatile society. The brotherhoods, a feature of Sufi mysticism, cut across ethnic, family, and class divides. Generally centered on the life and teachings of a respected historic figure, whose contemporary descendent demanded strict discipline and tithing from members, they provided what such fraternities offer anywhere. Under a general statement of beliefs and a code of personal conduct, they offered social cohesiveness, the glue of belonging in otherwise fluid societies. Extended family ties remained important, but the brotherhoods provided a place to be at home, friendship, economic and psychological support, assistance in time of need, a presence at life's entrances and exits, and a positive identity in an often-disrupted society. In a wider context, they represented a buffer zone of stability that has allowed Senegal to escape the Jacobean flareups and riots that have erupted in other African countries.[13]

There is little difference between the two main brotherhoods, Tijaniya and Mouridiya, ritually or organizationally. Both are hierarchical and, in each case the founder and his successors claim a chain of authority or a genealogy linking them to the Prophet or to the earliest years of Islam. Disputes emerge occasionally within communities, largely over succession issues, or between brotherhoods over a political or economic issue, but both have proven resilient and adaptable. Senegalese Islamic disputes rarely become violent.

The Mouridiya

Pray as if you will die tomorrow, but work as if you will live forever
—Cheikh Amadou Bamba, founder of the Mouride Brotherhood

The Mouridiya, founded by a charismatic and well-organized leader, Amadu Bamba (1850–1927), took advantage of Senegal's disrupted society in the immediate postjihad era. As warriors departed or were defeated and their followers sought communities to join, the Mouridiya was there and soon numbered over 70,000 adherents.

Bamba attracted those displaced and uprooted by the French conquest, defeated and displaced soldiers and peasants. Soon they developed a compound and established a prayer life and a hierarchy unyieldingly dependent on its founder's absolute control. Its rule of life stressed positive thinking and hard work, mutatis mutandis the Islamic version of the Protestant ethic. Mouride control of the groundnut industry and transportation networks were preludes to its gradual overseas expansion toward the century's end. Young Mouride vendors could be found hawking fake Rolex watches on the Grand Canal of Venice or driving vans along the interstates in America, loaded with African art, which they would sell at street corners and then return home, to emerge later with another shipment.[14]

In recent years, power has gradually devolved to the highly centralized and tightly disciplined Mouridiya, which is of local Senegalese origins and which represents an interesting amalgam between indigenous and imported religious practices. Its autocratic founder, Amadu Bamba, rejected Arab religious authority and required his followers to make a yearly pilgrimage to his capital, Touba. Now Senegal's second-largest city, it draws over a million pilgrims a year and is fast becoming an ecological wasteland. Since the colonial period, the originally rural-based brotherhood has held a monopoly of the peanut trade, Senegal's principal export, and virtually controls the public transport sector. Its strong political influence and social capital generated by skillful networking allows the brotherhood to move from strength to strength. At home its members receive preferential access to trade, and their international commercial networks—almost a multinational corporation—now extend to Europe and the United States, funding purchases of large tracts of land in Senegal. Its members enrich the brotherhood through regular voluntary contributions (*hadiya*).

The Mouridiya is attracting city migrants, expatriate Senegalese traders and business persons, and members of the middle class who are critical of government corruption. As a result, its outlook is changing from that of an inward looking, once-rural religious sect to that of the country's most dynamic political and religious force, one with diverse economic interests. The brotherhood's membership may be 4 million, slightly under half the national population, and its power and prestige were enhanced by the election of an active Mouride member, Abdulaye Wade, as Senegal's president.

The Tijaniya

Founded by an Algerian cleric and brought to the western Sahara by a Mauritanian missionary, the Tijani Sufi mystical movement was carried throughout the Senegambia in the early nineteenth century by El Hajj Umar Tall. Its leading exponent was Malik Sy (c. 1855–1922), a Wolof, whose extended family was situated at his *zawiya* (center) in Tivaouane. Sy proved skilled at peaceful accommodation with the French, which allowed him to concentrate on teaching and leading a religious life. Villalón notes, "He won numerous followers among the Wolof, particularly in the new towns that were emerging along the railroad lines," and "the family continues to be one of the two most important maraboutic families in Senegal today."[15]

Another follower, the leader of the second influential *maraboutic* family, Ibrahim Niass (1900–1975) attracted a large following by emphasizing Sufi doctrines and the importance of modeling one's life on that of the Prophet. Excluding the "jihad of the sword," he preached the "jihad of the heart" and proclaimed himself the Savior of the Age. While in Mecca on a pilgrimage, he met the emir of Kano from Nigeria, who accepted Niass's leadership, thereafter, Niass sent emissaries all over West Africa, attracting large followings.

Niass was a modernist, an early user of tape recorders and audiocassettes, and he encouraged the active participation of women and children in religious services. The *marabout* was also a healer, and thousands flocked to him for prayers and protection against misfortune. With his prayers, the faithful believed that they would arrive in Paradise without having to face the Day of Judgment.

The Tijaniya is a loose federation of largely independent, often quarrelsome local branches and has been a seedbed for Islamist agitation during the past 20 years. The largely urban-based brotherhood controls several of Senegal's largest industries and staffs the government bureaucracy. The Tijaniya khalifes were active supporters of President Abdou Diouf, a Tijaniya loyalist. Membership in the order, once the largest of the Senegalese brotherhoods, is now estimated at 3 million, just under a third of Senegal's population of 9.9 million.

The Wahabi Reaction

Every religious movement calls forth a countermovement, and the progress of the brotherhoods did not go unchallenged. Reformers emerged, attacking what they regarded as excessive veneration of the Prophet; the elevation of brotherhood founders and leaders into an intermediary status between believers and God; the exploitation of followers for their money and labor; the use of local rituals, prayers, and music; and the venality and corruption of society.

Such reformist groups were broadly called Wahabi, named for Shaikh Muhammad b. Abdmal al-Wahab, an eighteenth century Central Arabia cleric, who helped establish the House of Saud. Aiming to restore Islam to its original pure form, he launched a Cromwellian purist's campaign against moral and religious laxity, the veneration of holy men and tombs, Sufism, any forms of magic or the occult, and the remnants of folk religion.

During the 1950s, the Ivory Coast became an important center of West African Wahabism, and the movement spread elsewhere, including to Senegal, where its numbers were never large but its followers were vocal. Although its stated aim was to unify the community, in its intensity and intransigence and its unyielding censorship of other movements it proved to be an unremitting source of division.

The French Policy: "Islam Noir"

French policy toward the brotherhoods was initially contradictory. Twice they exiled the Mouride's leader, Amadou Bamba, once to Gabon (1895–

1902), then to Mauritania (1903–1907), but this only succeeded in making him an increasingly popular hero. Eventually the French devised a policy of accommodation with the *grands marabouts* and allowed them to function as long as they did not oppose France. This, in turn, left them virtually free to pursue their commercial and religious activities. Roman Catholic missions, by government design and church agreement, kept largely to the coastal regions and the Serer and Diola non-Islamic regions.

France as a Muslim power was the work of French officers who served in Algeria, some with the Bureaux Arabes, where they learned the local language and customs to better enforce French policies.[16] Faidherbe had installed a Muslim Tribunal in 1857, followed by a school for training chiefs and interpreters, as well as the Tirailleurs Sénégalais infantry units, dressed in what the French imagined were Algerian or Ottoman uniforms. Muslim Affairs was moved directly under the Direction of Political Affairs, next door to the governor-general's office. By the 1890s, some of the French Arabist officers from Algeria were sent to West Africa, among them the brilliant Xavier Coppolani and Octave Depont, who made a thorough study of the brotherhoods and recommended ways for the French to coopt them as its agents. In 1892 an associate of Coppolani's argued that French policy toward the Sufi orders should make its leaders agents of the state, entrusted in certain circumstances to distribute assistance to the poor, manage schools, and administer areas around their *zawiya* (lodges): "With official titles and subsidies . . . with frequent visits and aid in the reconstruction of mosques and saints tombs . . . with confidence reestablished between the directors of Islam and the European regents, one could begin, with great delicacy, the work of improving Islam and moving it in the direction of our civilization."[17]

Beau Geste: The Twilight of the French Presence

The end of World War II left France unable to recoup its former powers in its overseas colonies, and by 1960 Senegal was independent. Although for several additional decades France remained a dominant European presence in the West African country, the glory days of the French-Senegalese *politique des drapeaux*—most visible in the Senghor–de Gaulle epoch— became a thing of the past.[18] In the early twenty-first century, despite a substantial economic presence, France was no longer the force it once was in Senegal. Diminished military, economic, and technical-educational resources to fund its African presence meant a reduced political influence as well. France was left with largely its cultural card to play, what remained of the *mission civilisatrice* and *la francophonie*. But here restrictive French immigration policies at home undid its cultural initiatives abroad. Young Senegalese who could be dissecting the writings of classic French authors instead were learning English and studying about computers and their global usage to find jobs in the country's emerging cyber communications industry or abroad.

French policy interests turned increasingly to Europe, especially to relations with Germany, and France was now less inclined to back its favored protégés among African rulers. Although French President Jacques Chirac was godfather to President Abdou Diouf's younger daughter, when Diouf was considered a liability France refused to continue to support him. This led to an open election, the aging leader's defeat, and his exodus to a fashionable Paris apartment.[19] With the 1997 passing of Jacques Foccard, éminence grise and adviser on African affairs to French presidents, his discreet Paris-Dakar-Bangui telephone networks fell into disuse. Finally, French involvement in recent Senegal–Guinea Bissau fighting revisited many themes from a distant expansionist past. President Chirac stoutly maintained that Paris had no dog in that fight, but France supported Dakar's efforts to end the insurgency and limit cross-border smuggling and support for the Diola Casamance rebels. Although France wanted to shore up Senegal's economy, drained for years by fighting with the rebels, the era of dispatching legionnaires or parachutists was long past and the dispute festered.

Christian-Muslim Relations, a Delicate Balance

The relationship between two major world religions, Islam and Christianity, is a potential source of stability and cooperation in Senegal, but in reality relations are more often characterized by mutual suspicion and competition. Christianity in Senegal is primarily Roman Catholic, accounting for less than 2% of the population, much of it centered in the coastal region. Although small in numbers, the church has exercised a strong presence in the country. President Senghor was a Catholic intellectual, and Dakar has long been a center for prestigious denominational schools, seminaries, institutions, and publications. In Senghor's time, visible efforts at Christian-Muslim dialogue took place, designed to contribute to the country's delicate equilibrium. What the future holds is conjecture, but both Muslim and Christian leadership is basically peaceful in nature, not seeking overt confrontation, and this may set the parameters for future interaction between the two groups.

Overview—Why Senegal Is Different

Senegal's contemporary political life is an amalgam of Islamic and Western institutions and perspectives. During the colonial period its role as the administrative capital of French West Africa (AOF) gave the country an importance out of proportion to its wealth and size and, at the time of independence, provided Senegal with a secular, democratic, and highly centralized form of government.

Then and now, Islamic institutions have been central to the country's political life. A large Muslim community has been a significant player in West African politics since the time of medieval Muslim empires, and Senegal's government relies on Islamic institutions to provide popular support and legitimacy. Senegalese politics is Muslim politics, and the symbols and language of Islam permeate the political arena. Store signs with the portraits of well-known Islamic leaders or names like Horlogerie d'Islam, Touba Restaurant, and Bamba Boutique, named for the Mouride founder, are widespread in Dakar streets, as are reverse-glass image-texts of individual revered figures, such as Amadu Bamba.[20] Numerous political-religious organizations and institutions flourish in the country, and there is little of the hostility toward the state's secular character expressed elsewhere in the Muslim world. In fact, a symbiotic, albeit often ambiguous, relationship exists between the government and Islamic leaders. The government needs the brotherhoods because they are powerful and efficient, whereas the brotherhoods rely on the state for political and economic patronage.

Structure of the Community

Throughout its long exposure to Islam and Western influences, Senegal's Muslim community has tenaciously held on to its indigenous roots. Senegal's population is virtually defined by the Sufi brotherhoods, each with its own political and economic profile. The two largest brotherhoods, the Mouridiya and the Tijaniya, are closely aligned with the central government, and this association has provided them with substantial economic benefits and a key role in policymaking at the national level.

Islam and the State

The delicate cooperative balance between the government and these powerful Muslim institutions has been central to the maintenance of Senegal's political stability. President Senghor, a Christian in an overwhelmingly (over 94%) Muslim country, manipulated the brotherhoods and bought their support by playing them off against one another. President Diouf took another approach, acting as synthesizer and intermediary among them and attempting to harmonize their interests, a policy followed by his 74-year-old successor, President Wade, who became chief of state on April 1, 2000. Diouf had supported a national council of brotherhoods intended to meet collegially with one another and with government officials. Through power sharing, he drew a cross section of political and religious groups into an "expanded" administration.

Wade followed a similar policy. Although he campaigned on a platform of *sopi*, Wolof for "change," Senegal's limited political possibilities gave him little margin for effecting change, despite his winning both the presidential and legislative elections. Wade had made several visits to Touba, dressed in flowing white robes, and prostrated himself before the khalife while national television recorded the event. Both he and the Moslem leader vowed to stay in close contact, and the aged khalife voiced nuanced support for the president but declined to publicly ask for favors or endorse a legislative agenda.

Support from conservative Muslim leadership has enabled the government to survive the violent growing pains of a democratic process and allowed it to take balanced positions on controversial international issues while maintaining internal stability in a dangerously unstable region. The government's close relationship with Sufi leadership has helped keep the country independent of its more aggressive Arab neighbors despite Senegal's location on the volatile fault line between Arab and sub-Saharan Africa. Brotherhood leaders mediated violent disputes with Mauritania during the 1990s and fended off too close an association with Iran and Libya. Senegal closed the Iranian Embassy in 1984, accusing the Iranians of spreading "fundamentalist propaganda."[21]

The effort of Ahmed Niass, descendent of a venerable Tijaniya family, to found an Iranian and Libyan–influenced Hizboulahi (Party of God) political movement in 1979 came to naught. Its opportunistic founder, the self-styled "Ayatollah of Kaolack" (a town in South-Central Senegal) fled the country but was allowed to eventually return if he promised to stay out of politics.[22] Finally, the Muslim community's conservatism has allowed Senegal to strengthen ties with the West while seeking Middle East and North African financial support for the country. A main foreign connection for Senegalese Islam is with Morocco, which sent monetary and educational support to Senegal, reflecting its generally conservative brand of Islam, which emphasizes historical and cultural ties and good works. Moroccans and Senegalese point with pride to Islam's eleventh-

century arrival in Senegal from Morocco and the nineteenth-century Tijaniya brotherhood, which can trace its origins to the Moroccan holy city
of Fez. In 1955, on his return from exile in Madagascar, Mohammed V
of Morocco stopped in Dakar to thank Seydou Nourou Tall, a local Tijaniya leader, who supported him against the French. On March 27, 1964,
Hassan II of Morocco dedicated the Grand Mosque of Dakar, built with
Moroccan funds and workers.[23]

Militant Islamist groups, generally from the Tijaniya but oriented toward developments elsewhere in the Muslim world, have so far failed to
take substantial root in Senegal and remain junior members of the larger
brotherhood organizations. They have not attracted a broad following and
have moved away from Middle East radicals in recent years; they now
focus their efforts mainly on Tijaniya succession politics and education.

The Moustarchidine wal Moustarchidaty, a militant Tijaniya student
group, played a prominent role in violent demonstrations over economic
issues in 1994 but failed to gain more than a small student following. The
Young Mourides' association, a group of university students that defend
Mouride beliefs against Tijaniya and secular influences, has attempted to
extend beyond the university campus to a broader youthful audience in
Senegal's cities but remains under the control of the Mouride leadership.

Ironically, the role of the Sharia, so contentious in several African
states, never became a significant issue in Senegal. The major brotherhoods never endorsed it, although fundamentalists made an effort to institute Sharia and remove the word *secular* from the Senegalese constitution. When a "code of family law" was adoped in the 1960s, the Muslim
brotherhoods mobilized against the Senghor government, but the code
that was finally adopted, according to Babou, "did not affect the life of
the majority of Senegalese who continued to manage their family according to Muslim law and tradition."[24]

Problems Facing the Community

However, the Muslim establishment's close identification with government policies is a source of weakness for the community as both Islamic
and government leaders seek to deal with the same socioeconomic problems, including the following:

- Succession to aging leadership: the brotherhoods face the prospect
  of changing leadership. The 83-year-old Mouride Khalife, son of
  the order's founder, is ailing. His only brother and successor is 71
  years old. All members of the Mouridiya leadership signed a bind-

ing agreement in 1952 that stipulated that succession to the title would pass to the khalife's younger brothers before a third generation would have a chance to rule. Although the present khalife is still able to unite the whole brotherhood for a yearly celebration, other leadership centers are appearing with their own celebrations and local pilgrimages. Succession within the Tijaniya promises to be more immediately complicated, with no clear line to the khalifate in the two different subbrotherhoods. The Niass completed a successful transmission of power in recent years, but intense rivalries for positions of power remain.

- Urbanization, unemployment, and youthful delinquency: the Senegalese economy, with one of the highest gross national products (GNPs) in West Africa, continues to profit from its economic ties to France, but it has not provided enough jobs for a population that is growing at 2.7% yearly in a country where unemployment is at 40%.[25] Over 40% of Senegal's population has moved to the cities, seeking to escape the economic stagnation of the countryside or to find employment after graduation from schools and universities. One-half of them now live in Dakar, and 25% are unemployed. Young migrants "without family or faith" are creating a serious crime problem and a related drug scene. To conservative Islamists, this new "TV generation" no longer fits into traditional Muslim social categories. They say it is exemplified by the Baye Fall, a group created by a disciple of Amadu Bamba, the founder of the Mouridiya, that has become a gathering point for distraught urban youths. The group has become more than a nuisance, modeling itself on the Rastafarians, roaming Dakar's streets in tattered garments and rastas, and aggressively begging and attacking people they identify as "bad Muslims."

- Destructive agricultural practices: environmental degradation is an acute problem in Senegal. The agricultural sector, undermined by desertification, is stepping up migration from the countryside to the cities. Exploitative land management policies responsible for the Mourides early economic successes are destroying significant portions of Senegal's arable lands and threaten the future of the country's agricultural sector. Such practices have turned the Mouride capital region around Touba into a wasteland and have serious environmental implications for land that the Mourides are acquiring elsewhere in the country.

- Social tensions: caste and class tensions within the brotherhoods, in the past ignored by the elite, affect brotherhood solidarity and complicate brotherhoods' political activities, which went unquestioned in the past. More than half the Senegalese population is descended from slaves and other low-caste groups and continues to be subordinated by noble families that control both political and religious hierarchies. Within the Tijaniya, for example, the khalife is a member of the noble Sy family, whereas the political and religious leaders of junior branches descend from the lower-caste Niass family. "The Niass has never been subordinate and do not consider themselves to be under the authority of the Sy," Babou observes.[26] Poorer members of noble families, resentful of the wealth accumulated by nouveau riche members of lower caste groups, also demand radical religious and economic reforms to remedy their situation. An added source of stress is the conflict produced by aging leadership at the top of the main brotherhoods; as numbers of adherents increase gradually and there is little room at the top, individual religious leaders leave and gather their own followings.

The Balance Upset

Probably the greatest present challenge to both the Muslim community and government is the rapidly increasing power of the Mouridiya at the expense of the Tijaniya, which has been weakened by the factional social tensions. Once equal in number, the Mourides are attracting members from core Tijaniya groups and from Senegal's growing urban populations. The Mouridiya doctrine of salvation by labor provides a spiritual anchor for its urban following and reinforces the bonds that tie traders in Italy, Germany, France, and the United States to the brotherhood's center in Touba. The Mouridiya's rapid growth, its increasing economic successes, and above all its acquisition of land in and around the Senegal Valley, the traditional Tijaniya heartland, worries Tijaniya leaders and has provoked violent attacks on Mouride interlopers by Tijaniya members.

Analysis and Conclusion

The balanced relationship between the Dakar government and the Muslim brotherhoods is changing. The government's ability to balance the interests of the powerful Muslim brotherhoods has been in large measure responsible for Senegal's peaceful postindependence transition. Presidents Senghor, Diouf, and Wade exerted leverage over the brotherhoods because the latter were fairly equally balanced in size and power. As a result, the Mouridiya's increased wealth and power has important implications for Senegal's carefully maintained political-religious balance. Also, the government's ability to govern will be hampered if they become even stronger. Without the power to play the brotherhoods off against one another or to encourage their cooperation, the state's ability to maintain civil order, engineer a peaceful presidential succession, reduce crime, jump-start the economy, shore up the deteriorating environment, and ease social tensions will be markedly reduced. Since 1993, the Mouride Khalife no longer instructs his followers to vote for the president and ruling Socialist Party, fearing he will lose support himself from substantial numbers of followers in the political opposition.

The Mourides encourage the notion that the area around Touba is virtually independent of Dakar's governance. They have expelled customs officials and run an extensive smuggling operation unchallenged by national authorities, have closed government schools that compete with their own Islamic educational system, and have felt free to appoint and dismiss local government officials. Yet growth and success bring their own problems. Babou notes, "The development of the holy city of Touba and the brotherhood as a whole is bringing new challenges that the hierarchy of the brotherhood has failed to address correctly," specifically the need for effective public administration to face such issues as security and sanitation. Three years ago the brotherhood appointed a *griot* (praise singer) as city manager. Local traders objected to his efforts to collect taxes to pay for the needed improvements, but "a great number of people supported the decision."[27]

Moreover, pressing social tensions will challenge the Muslim community's leadership in the next few years. Not only are the Tijaniya divided by generational and class differences and competition for leadership, but also there are latent signs that the Mouridiya itself could face internal differences, as might be expected in a growing organization with aging leadership. Occupational groupings within the Mouride population are appearing. Professional groups that attract intellectuals, lawyers, and business representatives meet to discuss national issues. Associations of Mouride expatriates in Europe and the United States are increasingly influential within the brotherhood and are likely to become less submissive to authoritarian control from Touba, whose religious leadership they respect but whose political directives they no longer loyally follow.[28]

Brotherhood leaders probably have less reason to be concerned about the future of an Islamist movement in Senegal than they did in the 1980s immediately following the Iranian revolution.[29] Despite intense efforts to bring fundamental change to Senegal's sturdy Sufi brotherhood system, Islamist numbers remain few and their organizations fragmented and weak. But if traditionally conservative Tijaniya authorities are further weakened, it will give greater scope to Islamist doctrine, rejecting the authoritarian intermediary role of Sufi *marabouts* between the faithful and God.

The importance of Senegal to Western policymakers remains out of proportion to its size and economic strength. Since independence, it has maintained a position of political stability and middle-of-the-road policies in a continent torn by violence and in an international Muslim community troubled by religious extremism. This has been underlined by visits from American and French heads of state, by continuing foreign assistance from Western countries, and by the maintenance of a French military base in Senegal despite the reduction of French forces elsewhere in Africa. Following the September 11, 2001, terrorist attacks in America, President Wade called for the creation of a multifaceted African pact against terrorism, part of a global effort "to team up with the world coalition against terrorism." The state would agree not to indulge in terrorist acts or to allow terrorists to function from their territories. A body of inspectors would be created to verify compliance. Meanwhile, greater security at airports, borders, ports of entry, and on streets was called for.[30]

The Muslim community is critical to Senegal's continued moderation and stability. The brotherhoods' conservative leadership has seen that it has everything to gain by a mutually supportive relationship with secular authorities, and a new generation of leadership may very well read its best interests similarly once in power. Nevertheless, changing political dynamics within both of the principal Sufi orders have reduced the Mouride Khalife's open political role. They have also brought Islamic reformists closer to leading the Tijaniya, who may exert a new, less moderating influence on Dakar's policies within the next decade.

Eastern Approaches

*Islam as a Minority Religion
in Kenya*

From earliest times Muslims were a visible presence along the Indian Ocean of East Africa, often called the Swahili coast for the language spoken there.[1] A thriving Muslim community governed the island of Zanzibar, and along the coast there were Islamic fishing, farming, and trading communities, the rhythm of their life determined by the annual monsoon winds and the maritime trade, which brought and sent people and goods to and from India, the Far East, and the Arabian Peninsula.

From Earliest Times: Differing Interests

No single Muslim presence extended throughout the coast; what existed was an archipelago of communities, sometimes cooperating but just as often isolated from one another. And even later, when Islam had spread to the interior, its internal divisions prevented it from presenting a unified front. There was a geographic split, the coast versus the interior, with "Arab" light-skinned residents of the former voicing disdain about dark-skinned "African" inhabitants of the latter. And inland the largest Islamic concentration was near the Somali border, a region with a geographical and cultural affinity with neighboring Somalia rather than with Kenya. Doctrinal differences separated the communities as well. Whereas most Kenyan coastal Muslims were tolerant and moderate in outlook, within Kenya the Islamist versus modernist split was real and rivalries among individual Islamic leaders were pronounced. Most were regarded by their constituencies as speaking for themselves rather than for the community. Meanwhile, Kenya's postindependence political leaders proved adroit at divide-and-rule politics, constantly frustrating the minority Islamic community by using its people at election time but otherwise leaving them resentful outsiders in their own country.[2]

A Flourishing Islamic Coastal Culture

Islam came early to the region, brought by traders from India and the Arabian Peninsula, and it expanded gradually and peacefully from the tenth to the fifteenth centuries. It became the dominant religion of the coastal people, who still retained many indigenous religious practices, such as local architectural styles for mosques, ritual scarification, and amulet making.[3] After the Portuguese Christian invaders (1500–1800) were defeated, the Islamic presence expanded. Links with the Middle East were strengthened, and the Arabization of local cultures was extended. Migrations from Yemen, the Indian Ocean, and the western Sudan increased, and with commercial prosperity came support for Islam. A rich coastal literature developed, encouraged by Hadhrami immigrants from southern Arabia. By the seventeenth century an extensive body of poetry in the Swahili language was in existence, much of it centered in neighboring Somalia. It would prove to be a major contribution to world literature.

Later an improved commercial economy, derived principally from the slave trade, as well as other, long-distance trading, gave local rulers the means to build mosques, establish Koranic schools, and employ religious scholars. No effort was expended to make such services available to women or nonprivileged people.[4]

In addition to Zanzibar and Mozambique, with its 30 mosques, Pate, a small island off Kenya's northern coast, became an important center for both coastal and coastal-inland trade, for Islamic learning, and for the growing slave and ivory trades. It was also the home of several influential Muslim scholars and was the base of resistance to Christianity. Portuguese priests were poisoned and churches desecrated. By the early nineteenth century, Portuguese influence faded on the East African coast, and the Arabization of culture proceeded apace. Sultan Said ibn Sultan (1832–1856) moved his capital from Muscat in Oman to Zanzibar, and the island increased its importance as a center for trade.[5] The Zanzibar sultans also established an elaborate system of qadi courts, and pilgrims were encouraged to make the hajj.

Islam Moves Inland

Islam moved inland in Kenya and surrounding countries during the nineteenth century, its original penetration slowed by the difficult inland passage. Kenya's Swahili coast, known locally as the Mrima coast, was a stretch of land 500 miles long, extending from the Tana to the Rufiji River. For part of the region, the fertile coastland extended fewer than 20 miles inland, followed by dry, inhospitable scrubland before becoming the lush highlands that attracted colonial settlement and plantations. Islam was thus slow to enter the interior, and coastal life gravitated toward the sea and the bustling Zanzibar sultanate. Several small, independent Islamic communities existed along the coast, but no wider state ever emerged.

By the mid-nineteenth century, long-distance caravans regularly visited the interior, and agricultural trade expanded between coastal Muslims and interior grain farmers. And as the slave trade declined under European pressure, traffic in foodstuffs increased; some of the demand was for grain to feed domestic slaves still held on Zanzibar clove plantations. (Plantation and household slavery remained a feature of the region, despite its formal abolition by the European powers, and both slaves and their owners were Muslims, something Christians would constantly cite over the next century.) Cooper suggests the presence of from 15,000 to 20,000 slaves each year on Zanzibar in the mid-nineteenth century, totaling $120,000 in revenues for 1861–1862: "Slave trading, for both local use and export, was a big business. It remained that way until effective antislave trade measures were finally taken in the 1870s."[6] Romero discusses several forms of domestic and household slavery in Zanzibar in coastal cities like Lamu in the 1950s.[7]

Growing trade brought expanded settlement, and coastal Muslims moved gradually inland, encountering local people, some of whom accepted the new faith, often melding it with traditional practices. What Sperling has called "rural Islamization"[8] became a feature of late nineteenth-century Islamic expansion, as was the presence of two main brotherhoods, the Qadiriya and the Shadhiliyya, but they never became the important forces they were in neighboring Tanzania.[9] The largest brotherhood, the Qadiriya, came to Zanzibar from Somalia in 1884, but its influence in Kenya was minimal. The much smaller Alawiyya brotherhood was a limited presence in Lamu and does not appear to have expanded elsewhere.[10] Traders were, above all, traders, not missionaries, and their extended routes did not mean that an immediate conversion to Islam followed. What appears to have occurred was a slow, subtle process:

an Islamic community grew and found a teacher; then some local people, principally through their chiefs, joined the community, bringing with them remnants of their traditional religions, which gave local Islam a distinct coloration.[11] Often the agents of change were artisans, carpenters, metalworkers, masons, and goldsmiths.[12]

Colonial Policy: Indirect Rule

No coherent Islamic policy was ever formulated by the Germans, whose East African presence ended with their defeat in World War I, or the British, who stayed until independence in 1963. Nevertheless, colonialism deeply influenced the course of East African Islamic history, principally through the introduction of Christian missionaries after 1860. The diffusion of Islam to Kenya's interior came from the inland expansion of coastal traders, as well as from the new railway from Mombasa to the interior, completed in 1902. In colonial times, the British employed a system of indirect rule, retaining local rulers, whom they brought under British control and placed on the government's payroll. The colonial capital moved inland to Nairobi in 1907, further contributing to the coastal-inland split.

Initially, Muslims were appointed as clerks and tax collectors and as chiefs by the Germans and British, but gradually that changed as educated Christians emerged from mission schools. By the 1920s Roman Catholic and Protestant missions were widespread throughout Kenya. Traditional Koranic teachers, around whom the Muslims rallied, proved no match for the expanding Christian missionary schools, which produced a rising generation of literate Kenyan leaders. When educational opportunities were offered to coastal people, Muslim parents resisted sending their children to secular or Christian schools. Also, many of the troops originally employed by both the Germans and British were Muslim. They moved about East Africa with the colonists, and many settled near the administrative centers to which they had been assigned, helping to create a small Islamic presence in scattered inland settlements.

Coastal Swahili Muslims both disliked manual labor and rarely acquired the fluency in English needed to be competitive in the newly emerging society. At the same time, they voiced contempt for the up-country Christians who were moving into positions of power in the colonial administration.[13] Muslims soon became marginalized, and the tensions between them and the ascendant Christians remained a sore point in subsequent relations between the two communities:[14]

By the time of the First World War, Muslim communities existed in or near most colonial administrative centers. Most of these communities inherited the dominant attributes of Swahili Islam (Sunni and the Shafi'i school of law), and they came to exhibit common underlying characteristics derived from Swahili coastal culture, notably Swahili cuisine, dress, dances and songs, and the use of Swahili as the language of Islam, though they continued to speak their vernacular language in daily life and in dealings with their non-Muslim fellow Africans.[15]

A century later, as Kenya's Muslim presence struggled for numbers and influence, its members looked back on an imagined golden era. Some Muslims of the coast province, seeing few government resources or jobs coming their way, attempted a short-lived political alignment with Zanzibar, the Mwambo ("coast" in Swahili) movement, which never succeeded.[16]

The Problems of Somali Muslims

The 600,000 Somalis of Kenya's northeastern province, ethnically and linguistically a part of Somalia but now in Kenya because of the vagaries of colonial partitioning, engaged in a lengthy, violent, and unsuccessful secessionist struggle.[17] Part of the Northern Frontier District (NFD) in British colonial times, the Somalis, mostly camel herders or cowherders— who claimed descent from the tribe of the Prophet Mohammed—stood by the results of a 1959 referendum, when their province voted to leave Kenya and become part of Somalia. After 1963, ethnic Somalis practiced guerilla warfare in a vain attempt to break away from Kenya, resulting in brutal clashes with security forces for the next four years. Governmental resources have been minimally allocated to the region, even though the Somali population is nominally represented in the cabinet and Parliament as recipients of the government's patronage to various ethnic groups.[18] Claims of second-class citizenship are similar to those voiced by coastal Arabs. The region is far behind the rest of the country. Illiteracy is at 87% in one district, infant mortality is several times higher than the national average,[19] and female genital mutilation remains a widespread practice. A contentious issue has been government demands that ethnic Somalis produce two forms of valid identification to receive passports. Muslims say that this is discrimination; the government claims it is to deter illegal immigration.[20]

Friction has been a constant feature of government and Somali Muslim relations. In July 1997, a provincial commissioner in the northeastern

province complained of a rising tide of Islamic fundamentalism. The specific issue was the standoff between the Islamic community and a district
commissioner over the licensing of 13 bars in Wajir, an action supported
by the courts. The government official said Muslim leaders in refugee
camps were fomenting discord throughout the region.[21]

Islamic Percentage of the Population

Kenyan Islam is divided along structural, geographical, ethnic, personality,
and doctrinal lines. Even as its numbers increased, it remained a sharply
divided community. A stratified Islamic society emerged, as did the rest
of Kenyan society, along ethnic and religious lines. In the Islamic in-
stance, the layers include Badawis, Baluchis, Bohras, Somalis, and Swahili
"Arabized" and "African" Muslims, all living in proximity but with minimal interaction. The divisions J. S. Furnvall saw in Mombasa held true
for other places as well: "The medley of peoples . . . mix, but do not combine. . . . As individuals they meet, but only in the market places, in buying and selling . . . different sections of the community [live] side by side,
but separately, within the same political unit. Even in the economic
sphere there is a division of labour along racial lines."[22]

The Islamic presence in Kenya is numerically small; by 1998 the number of Muslims was estimated at 5 million, possibly 20% of the country's
population,[23] whereas the Christian community represented 70% of the
population. Accurate numbers are hard to come by. One source, which
cannot be verified, listed the numbers of Kenyan Muslims as 100,000 in
1900, or 3.4% of the population, and 681,016 in 1962, or 7.9% of the
population.[24] Originally, most Kenyan Muslims came from the East African coast, but by the 1990s more than half of them were of Somali origin.
In the coast province, Muslims were 30% of the population and as high
as 50% in key coastal cities like Mombasa.

Asian Muslims, mostly from India and Pakistan, accounted for 176,000
persons in 1962, on the eve of independence, and were the backbone of
local economies wherever they settled. They included approximately
18,000 Shia Muslims from India's state of Gujarat, the majority of whose
ancestors were imported to work on the railroad in the late 1890s and
who later became core elements of the local business community.

Shiite Ismailis, followers of the Aga Kahn, numbered more than 10,000
in the 1970s and were an influential economic presence in Kenya. They
wore western dress, took out Kenyan citizenship, were generally prosperous, and stayed out of local politics. Loyal to the government in power,

they currently engage in philanthropic works, and their leader has easy access to the country's president. The Aga Khan Hospital in Nairobi is among the best medical institutions in the country.[25] The Aga Khan's investments also include a health chain, insurance company, real estate, newspapers, and the Diamond Trust of Kenya, which provides Ismailis with low-interest home loans.

A much smaller, 3,000–4,000 member sect was the radical Ithna'ashria (the Twelvers), whose religious orders came from Iran and Iraq. They established bookshops and schools in several cities and still support a theological seminary near Mombasa, from which they send promising students to Iran.[26]

Other Kenyan Islamic groups included the Badawi, a Shia clan of Yemeni immigrants that actively supported independence for coastal Muslims. A radical group, its members also participated in the 1987 Mombasa riots and reputedly had Libyan and Iranian ties. The Baluchi were of Iranian-Afghan origins yet were a conservative, anti-Khomeini Sunni group. The 7,000-member Bohras community represented an independent segment of Shia Muslims. An apolitical group of Indian origin, its spiritual leader was the dai-el-Mutlaq, who claimed descent from the Prophet and his son-in-law. Most Bohras were Kenyan citizens, active in commerce, but they interacted largely with others in the Bohra community.

Kenya Muslims, unlike South African Muslims, were not all well educated and well placed in the professions. Muslims complained that proselytizing Christians ran the country's educational system. Muslim parents preferred to send their children to mosque schools, where the staple was learning the Koran by heart. A wide network of such *madrasas* extended into rural areas.[27] Older students in these schools learned about Muslim law (*fiqh*) and tradition (*hadith*) but no secular subjects, such as English, science, or mathematics, were taught. Some sheikhs forced parents to remove their children from public schools.[28] A few more advanced schools emerged, and the Riyadha Mosque College (1889) became the main source of educating local religious leaders; the Madrasatul Munawarrah School (1990) in Nairobi attracted over 700 students.

National Politics: A Minority Presence

Muslims have been a distinct minority presence in national politics. The Kenyetta and Moi cabinets, drawn largely from Kikuyu and Luo constituencies, gave no places to Muslims until 1982, but in 1987 Kenya Muslims won 7 seats in Parliament out of 170; in 1992 the number would rise to

24 deputies. Ronald Ngala, although not a Muslim, was from coastal Kilifi and chaired the Kenyan African National Union Party (Kanu Party) in the late 1960s. Ngala skillfully played intraparty differences to the advantage of his coastal region, but following his death in 1972 no comparable Muslim politician with national standing and requisite skills emerged. By the century's end, a Muslim was usually named a cabinet minister, and some became junior ministers in less influential positions. Of the 40 to 50 ministers and assistant ministers, 2 or 3 positions might go to Muslims, usually drawn from a small circle of party loyalists.[29] Muslim deputies were often criticized for being more interested in taking care of themselves than of their wider Muslim constituency. On the other hand, the constituency was sorely divided in outlook, and widely spread out across the country as well.[30]

Kenyan Muslims, despite an advantageous geographical location, had only limited exchanges with North Africa and the Arabian Peninsula and never established Islamic universities or centers of learning. Kenyan Islam was consequently heavily conservative and rigid in it opposition to modernizing influences. The community was outspoken against innovation or modernization but sometimes launched evangelizing missions (dawa), emulating Christian ones, but with little success. They had also conducted a crude disinformation campaign, clandestinely circulating the spurious Gospel of Barnabas, a Middle Ages forgery that has Jesus endorsing Mohammed as the true prophet.[31]

Internal Divisions: Geographical, Doctrinal, Racial

Islam in Kenya has been internally divided. The focal point for individual Muslims is the mosque and its imam. Local imams teach and preach and in turn receive financial support from a network of the faithful. Rivalries are a feature among imams in such a setting, and making common cause with colleagues is infrequent. The Kenyan Muslim leadership rallied to condemn Salman Rushdie's The Satanic Verses,[32] a safe target, and denounced the active Christian presence in Kenyan education and politics, but personality and structural differences work against any closer forms of cooperation.

Doctrinal Differences: The Conservative-Modernist Divide

Many older conservatives resist change, believing that forms of worship should remain unaltered, Muslim children should not attend public schools, women should not be educated, and arranged marriages should be the norm. The chief *qadi* of Kenya, Shaikh al-Amin Mazrui, an outspoken opponent of modernization until his death in 1968, was followed by successors who promoted a return to stricter, Salafi forms of Islam and opposed veneration of saints, costly celebrations at marriages and deaths, and the incorporation of folk practices into Islamic rituals.[33] Progressives believe that full educational and vocational opportunities should be available to women. They also oppose arranged marriages and elaborate, costly feasts, such as week-long wedding or funeral celebrations, worship at saints' tombs; and sustained public displays on the Prophet's birthday.

Another example of the internal conflict that divides Kenya's Muslim community concerns the starting and ending dates of Ramadan, the Muslim month of fasting. Who is responsible for setting the date? The chief *qadi* is, by tradition, but by the 1980s other leaders declared different dates.[34] When Shaikh Ali Mohammed Shee became imam of Nairobi's largest mosque in the 1990s, he announced a different date than the one proclaimed by his rival, the chief *qadi*, whom he called a nonelected government "stooge."[35] (Since British times, the *qadi* has been a salaried government employee and the government's principal adviser on Muslim affairs, supported by a network of 15 regional *qadis*.)

The controversy took a new turn at Id al-Fitr, the end of Ramadan, which the government declared a national holiday 31 days after its start. The government said that it was necessary to announce a national holiday well in advance, but true believers argued that only a religious leader could make that determination, depending on when he spotted the new moon. Like ancient Christians quarreling over the date of Easter, it is the sort of nonnegotiable dispute designed to produce maximum friction within a religious community. Another comparable issue over which Kenyan Muslims quarreled was whether drums (tambours) could be used in a mosque service and whether the regular Friday prayers (*jum'a*) should be followed by additional afternoon prayers.[36] Such seemingly minor issues take on importance in already divided communities.

Racial Divisions

The historic Arab Muslim versus African Muslim split also contributes to a divided Muslim community. And within this divide comes coastal Swahilis, many of whom are a mixture of both groups while belonging to neither. The British made clear distinctions between Arabs and Swahilis, divisions soon ingrained into the country's life. The Swahilis feel humiliated by the Arabs and different from black Africans, the country's majority population. African Muslims argue that most of the major *qadi* positions go to Arab Muslims.

A dispute has also split the small Shiite community from the larger Sunni one. An outspoken opponent of the Shiites was Shaikh Ahmad Msallam, who studied in Iraq and who preached against what he called the Shia heresy. He was answered by Shaikh Abdullahi Nassir, a convert from the Sunni camp, who preached about the compatibility of the two systems in lectures that were widely spread about the country by cassette tapes.[37]

Personality Differences

Kenya Islam has splintered along personality, as well as doctrinal, lines. The grand *qadi*-imam rivalry of Nairobi's central mosque was followed by a no less costly split in Mombasa between Sharif Nassir, a local politician of Arab origin, and the Islamic community there. A combative personality, Nassir was an early outspoken Moi supporter, known locally as "President Moi's watchdog," for which he was rewarded with power and wealth. Both a member of Parliament and a Kanu Party loyalist, Nassir's heated struggles with Muslim opponents for public office left the coastal community divided.[38] One opponent, Abdallah Ndovo Mwidau, a former mayor of Mombasa, was removed from his job, and others were bruised by sharp personal attacks. Nassir won his parliamentary and party races by small margins, with the president's backing, but left a divided community in his wake.[39]

Stabs at Organization: Supkem, IPK, and UMA

From time to time, Kenyan Muslims made half-hearted efforts at uniting, but unity was never a feature of Islam in Kenya. A Supreme Council of Kenya Muslims (Supkem) was founded in 1973 but was a largely ineffectual forum.[40] It claimed to represent nearly 100 Muslim organizations, many of them with only a handful of members, and on paper at least had governing, provincial, and district councils. Several significant Islamic communities, however, especially coastal ones, refused to join it.[41] A government-front organization, Supkem had little creditability among the faithful. Its declared loyalty was to the president and the Kanu Party, and there was little contact between the leadership and its constituency in the organization's early years.[42] When violent riots broke out between rival Muslim groups in Mombasa in 1992–1994, Supkem could play no mediating role: "Supkem's influence on religion, society, and politics seems to be much smaller than its announcements would lead one to believe."[43] Supkem received funds from other countries, including the Sudan, Egypt, Libya, Kuwait, and Saudi Arabia. Criticism that the organization's leaders were inefficient and corrupt was widespread, as was the lack of account-ability for funds received.[44]

In 1992 the Kenyan government announced that multiple political parties could now register. The Islamic Party of Kenya (IPK) was formed, based largely on Mombasa Muslims, some of whom were arrested by the government. The party gained few followers and was never registered by the government, which claimed it was a religiously affiliated party, a po-sition it consistently held despite vocal protests from the Muslim com-munity.[45] The party's main founders were Omar Mwinyi, a primary school teacher, and Abdul Rahman Wandati, an Islamic teacher. Its following came from Muslims who experienced discrimination in all aspects of pub-lic life, from seeing choice coastal land being increasingly awarded to up-country presidential supporters to being given only limited access to government-run radio and TV stations.[46]

The government's main strategy was to create the United Muslims of Africa (UMA) in May 1993, hoping to drive a wedge in the IPK's con-stituency. Tensions between the two organizations mounted. A conse-quence of the government's denial to Muslims of general political access was increased rioting in Mombasa, especially between June and July 1993, when petrol bombs were thrown and several persons were killed or in-jured. A deteriorating climate of public order resulted, with increased criminality, a decline in the important tourist industry (a main source of coastal revenue), and people fleeing the region.[47]

Muslims and Christians: An Enduringly Hostile Climate

The political climate Kenyan Muslims face is largely hostile, and Muslim-Christian relations are often tense as well. Name-calling and at times violence are features of Kenya's religious landscape. Christian numbers are roughly divided between Protestants and Catholics, with a growing num-ber of independent churches, one of the fastest-expanding movements in East Africa.[48] Denominational, leadership, ethnic, and regional rivalries split the Christian community as well. These divisions mirror those of the much smaller Islamic community, except that the Christians are in power through their hold on the government. It should not be suggested that either the Christian or Muslim presences are monochromatic; in fact, individual Christian leaders often take sharp issue with the government, sometimes paying for it with their lives, as did Anglican Bishop Alexander Muge, an outspoken critic of the misuse of power and of governmental corruption.[49]

Christian-Muslim grievances are deep-seated. The chief Muslim complaints are that Christian missionaries run the country's educational system, the government is in Christian hands, Christian judges do not respect Sharia law, and Muslims are constantly branded as former slave traders. The result is that Muslims are painted as ethnically and religiously marginalized strangers in their own land.[50] Particularly egregious for Muslims was a statement by Maurice Cardinal Otunga at a 1993 African Episcopal Conference in Nairobi, urging Christians to actively combat Islam since Muslims were attempting to turn Africa into an Islamic continent and to destroy Christianity.[51] After alarm was raised in the secular and religious press, the cardinal said that his remarks were aimed at Islamic fundamentalists, citing their calls for jihads against infidels. Eventually tensions diminished, but a climate of mistrust endures.

Tensions flared in July 1998 when an itinerant American evangelist named Edward Andrews Stagl attached posters to a mosque saying that the Prophet was an adulterer. Stagl was arrested and deported, but Muslims in the Rift Valley town where the incident occurred rioted, a church was burned, and illegal brew dens were destroyed. During the same period, a land row between Nairobi Muslims and their curio dealer neighbors erupted into violence. The downtown Jamia mosque had tried for years to expand into a nearby lot occupied by a number of merchants. The dispute was in court when, on the night of July 26, 1998, Muslims used bulldozers to clear the lot, flattening the dealer's kiosks, and ordered the occupants to move. Police refused traders access to their stands, which were then burned by unknown arsonists. Merchants retaliated by stoning the mosque, blocking its entrances, and burning pigs' heads as an insult to Muslims.[52]

On December 1, 2000, Muslim and Christian youths fought a running battle in Nairobi. The incident started when Muslim teenagers complained that wooden kiosks had been installed too close to a mosque. Kiosk vendors marched on the mosque; Muslims responded by burning a church and a seminary. A Roman Catholic church was burned as well, and when the Anglican archbishop was attacked by Muslim youths, Muslim leaders formed a human shield around him and led him to a hospital. More than 28 persons were admitted to hospitals on the first day of the riot.[53]

On the positive side, intermarriage does take place, although infrequently, between Christians and Muslims, and mosques and churches coexist peacefully on some Nairobi streets. When government security forces stormed All Saints' Cathedral in Nairobi in July 1997, where prodemocracy supporters were gathered, Christians and Muslims protested. Present at the large gathering was Shaikh Khalid Balala of the IPK, who had just returned to Kenya. Archbishop David Gitari acknowledged the Muslim leader's presence, and Balala was greeted with cheers. "Now the clamor for reforms is unstoppable," the Anglican prelate remarked.[54] The interfaith community also united to protest the president's plans to ask Parliament to review the Constitution rather than to open the constitutional discussion to the public, and police violently charged the peaceful demonstrators on June 10, 1999.

Radical Islam: Iran and Libya

The emergence of radical Islam in Kenya is in direct response to the situation of the Islamic community, in which Muslims are politically, economically, and demographically a minority people: "This appearance of militant groups is a common phenomenon throughout East Africa. It is, first and foremost, a symptom of the backwardness of Muslims in the economic, social, and political spheres and their strong sense of being discriminated against."[55]

Iran: Promoting Revolution

The success of the 1979 Iranian revolution spurred Islamists on, as did a new generation of believers who accepted a vision of the universal umma (community) different from that experienced in their native country.[56] The large Iranian Embassy in Nairobi has tried to widen the split between Kenya and Western nations over Kenya's lamentable human rights record and endemic corruption. Through publications, lectures, and mass media, it stresses the Iranian desire to restore Islam to its former glory, while attacking the "satanic forces" of imperialism and Zionism. The 1970s oil boom also increased the possibility of Arab funding of Islamic activities in Africa, for example, sending young Kenyans to Iran and elsewhere for study.[57]

Libya: a Closed Embassy

In 1981 the Libyan Embassy and Supkem organized a week-long gathering of Kenya Muslims. At that time Libya was sending both teachers to Kenya and up to 100 Kenyan students to Libya for study. The joint council's closing resolutions thanked "the brotherly leadership of Libya's Colonel Qadhafi for his help in promoting Islam around the world." Participants were urged to "arm themselves with more Arab and western education so they will have the ability to explain Islam to everyone in the world." Muslims were urged "to talk with their Christian brothers and sisters to show them the similarities between both religions in order to strengthen their confidence in Muslims."[58]

Kenya's leadership was not sympathetic to Muslims, and Kenya's Muslims did not provide a fertile ground for Libyan activities. The government had long suspected Libyans of being a source of unrest at Nairobi University. On November 4, 1987, while in Mombasa on the Prophet's birthday, President Moi attacked "religious fanatics" and "those who preach disunity, discord, and hatred." On December 20, Moi ordered the Libyan Embassy closed, and its staff was expelled from the country. "Libya-styled socialism" had no attraction for Kenya's one-party government.[59] More than a decade later, Kenyan Foreign Ministry officials indicated that Libya might reopen its embassy in Nairobi.[60]

The Bombing of the American Embassy

The bombing of the American Embassy in Nairobi on August 7, 1998, resulted in 250 deaths and 5,000 injuries. This embassy was apparently selected because it was a large, relatively unprotected building in a centrally located, easily accessible city space. Also, Kenya's porous borders and its seaports and airports allowed terrorists to enter with little difficulty. The terrorists came from outside of Kenya. Their external leader was Osama bin Laden. They included Wadid el Hage, bin Laden's former personal secretary, a Lebanese who lived in Khartoum before moving to Kenya in 1994, where he worked as a sometime gem dealer. Also included was Mohammed Saddiq Odeh, a Palestinian who trained terrorists in Somalia, then moved to Kenya in 1994. His cover was running a fishing business. Two others came from the Comoros Islands and from Yemen.[61] Most important, the terrorists could find cover and logistical support from the small, scattered Kenyan Islamic extremist community, although the country's mainstream Islamic leaders distanced themselves from the bombing. Supkem condemned the bombing, as did other Muslim groups, noting that 241 Kenyans lost their lives and that Islam was a religion of peace. The Sudan, long a home base to terrorist training groups, was suspected of links to the bombing, as was the large Iranian Embassy in Nairobi.[62] One consequence was a sweeping ban of Muslim nongovernmental organizations, and Federal Bureau of Investigation (FBI) and state security raids on Muslim organizations. Through court petitions, three of the five groups that had been deregistered were reinstated, but a climate of mistrust and hostility endured.[63]

Three years after the bombing, when the World Trade Center and the Pentagon were struck in America, Kenyans tied the two events together. Comments such as "Now America knows the same thing that happened here" and "So you got a real taste of it" were heard, in addition to many genuine expressions of condolences and support.[64] Following the attacks, thousands of angry Muslims demonstrated in Nairobi and Mombassa after Friday prayers. "Down with the US. . . . Osama is our hero," Nairobi crowds chanted at services presided over by Ahmed Mussallam, chair of Nairobi's Council of Imams and Scholars, who told the crowd, "Muslims are branded extremists only when they come out to defend justice."[65]

The Brief Political Career of Shaikh Khalid Balala

Shaikh Khalid Balala was an obscure market square preacher in Mombasa in 1992 when the Islamic Party of Kenya was formed, and within months the volatile, charismatic Islamic cleric became its de facto leader.[66] Billing himself as "the only Kenyan who gives President Moi nightmares," he delighted in president baiting and soon attracted himself unfavorably to the president and the police. Balala's brief, meteoric career as a politician ended within a few years. Its main result was to raise Kenyan Islamic issues on a national and international stage, even if their instigator could do little about them.

Born in 1958, the son of a Yemeni butcher, Balala spent over a decade in Saudi Arabia, studying at Medina University. Seizing on historic Kenyan Muslim discontent, he argued a conventional line: Muslims should pray, establish Koranic schools, and avoid foreign dress and the lures of tourism. Women must show moderation in dress and keep themselves "pure."[67]

For a while, the shaikh appeared to be a rising political star. Some opposition parties welcomed the IPK, believing they could coopt it in a coalition. But Balala, the loner, alienated as many people as he attracted,

and his political prospects dimmed when he accused Muslims in government of favoring their own private interests over those of the faithful.
Balala also unilaterally issued a *fatwa* (a legal decree) against moderate
Muslim leaders and told the press a core of suicide bombers stood by to
do his bidding.[68] Criticism within the party came swiftly. Opponents accused Balala of "hijacking" the party for his own purposes, of being a
publicity seeker rather than a leader, and of buying land with religious
contributions. In June 1994 he was expelled from the party.[69]

The government, meanwhile, frustrated Balala's plans by never allowing the IPK to register, by donating money to moderate Muslims, and by
encouraging individual Muslims to make the hajj—3,500 did in 1994,
and approximately 1,500 Kenyan Muslims make the pilgrimage annually.[70]
Also, the government increased the amount of local currency pilgrims
could exchange as a way of gaining favor.

In December 1994, while Balala was in Germany, the Kenyan government denied his routine application for a passport extension. By now the
politician was calling himself Shaikh General Balala and Simba (Lion)
Balala in media interviews.[71] He was finally permitted to return to Kenya
in 1997, where he continued his government baiting.[72] Once, when his
rhetoric flared up with a group of journalists, his mother warned, "I shall
stitch his mouth up unless he tones it down."[73]

Public rabble-rousing boomeranged on Balala at a Mombasa rally on
December 24, 1997, when a local crowd threatened to lynch him for
misleading Muslim youths, some of whom had been beaten and killed by
security forces in 1992.[74] Increasingly, the once listened to dissident figure
became an isolated self-publicist, waiting for interviews with a dwindling
number of journalists. In September 2001, Arye Oded observed, "During
my visit to Kenya this month I was told that he had no influence politically. I did not notice any sign of him."[75]

Issues in Sharia and Family Law

Questions of family law—particularly about inheritance—has been a
source of conflict between Muslims and the government. The Law of
Succession Act of 1972, an effort to sort out Kenya's numerous conflicting
practices, created a single legal code that incorporated common law, tribal
law, and the Sharia. But its provisions on marriage (monogamous vs. po-
lygamous), divorce, and inheritance produced no agreement.

Legal differences have had a long history in Kenya. A tripartite division
among legal systems originated in the East Africa order in Council of

1897. Like other law codes of the British Empire, it contained the controversial repugnancy clause, which voided any part of Islamic or traditional law repugnant to British morality, good conscience, and written law. Polygamy was declared such a repugnant practice, to the consternation of its Islamic practitioners.[76] A unique feature of the original decree was the designation of Kenya's coastal strip as a separate Islamic state within a wider jurisdiction. Similar provisions were contained in Kenya's 1963 Constitution.[77] A law on the structure of the courts was enacted, affirming the existence of Islamic courts but making them subordinate to the main common law courts.

The dispute between proponents of Sharia and the common law was particularly acute on issues of inheritance since the new law gave widows and female family members equal access to assets of the deceased. Kenyan law also required every citizen to have a will. Muslims claimed that the law was redundant since the Koran specified details of inheritances. When the government declared the law operational on July 1, 1981, Muslims protested. It did not help that Attorney-General Joseph Kamera said that the Sharia represented "outmoded" customs, much like tribal customs that must yield to progress. The Muslim response was swift and predictable: Sharia was God's law and should never be confused with tribal law.[78] President Moi publicly supported Muslims who sought an amendment to the law in 1990. Moi, an active Christian, told a goodwill delegation of Kenyan Muslims that the law of succession was contrary to the Koran and should be amended to satisfy Muslim demands.[79]

Conflict resumed in 1994 when the attorney-general said that the government was preparing a law that would allow women who were forced to have sexual relations with their husbands against their will to prefer rape charges. The leader of Nairobi's central mosque said that such a law opposed the spirit of the Koran and "damaged the institution of marriage and respect for it." By late 1999 the draft of the law had not been presented to Parliament.[80]

Conclusions

Islam represents a moderately growing minority political presence in Kenya, important at election times and in coalition politics. Geographical, doctrinal, and personality differences among Islamic leaders and communities prevent Muslims from presenting a solid political bloc. However, as the number of educated Muslims increases, so will an Islamic presence in public life.

Deep-seated Muslim perceptions of being a marginalized people will continue, and diminished economic prospects produce psychological frustration. Muslims complain that their few elected and appointed leaders favor their own interests, with little representation of the wider community. There are few indications that this will change.

Kenya has successfully contained radical Islam, especially with American security assistance in the postembassy bombing period. It remains a threat, however, since the root causes of societal discontent are unresolved. Islamists from the Sudan, Iran, and elsewhere will find enough receptivity to continue their activity because little has been done to address historic Muslim grievances of poverty, corruption, exclusion, and undue Christian political influence.

Tension will remain a feature of Muslim-Christian relations, to the detriment of all parties, unless rational voices prevail and make common cause among people of the book. Few such prospects are in the offing.

The place of Sharia law will remain in dispute, but nothing like the controversy in neighboring Sudan should engulf Kenya, where Muslims are a distinct minority and can live with compromise.

Different Currents

South Africa's Islamic Minority

The Congruence of Geography and History

The country's unique location helped shape the distinct character of Islam in South Africa. The maritime confluence of the South Atlantic and Indian Oceans and easy sea access north to the Suez Canal and the Arabian Peninsula allowed South Africa to be the recipient of Islamic settlers from Asia and the Islamic countries of North Africa and the Middle East. The Suez Canal's opening in 1869 and the advent of steamship passage to Zanzibar in 1910 facilitated such travel. Communication between South Africa and Egypt, Iran, and Saudi Arabia became important in the twentieth century when beleaguered South African Muslims looked beyond their borders for intellectual and revolutionary inspiration.

South African Islam was first of all local Islam. Its heart was in the activities of over 450 individual mosques, their imams, and their schools.[1] As such, it has been sharply divided for much of its history, hampered by geographical and structural differences. Its accomplishments are remarkable, despite the external and self-imposed obstacles, for it has produced some of the Islamic world's most articulate voices, martyrs, and holy people, as well as a vigorous community, in the face of daunting external pressures during the colonial and apartheid eras and the secularism of independent South Africa. South African Islam was also urban Islam because, though extensive in territory, 55% of South Africa's population lived in urban areas in 1966, as did most Muslims. The numbers of urban dwellers grew with independence and the lifting of residence restrictions, but the proportions changed little.[2]

South Africa's Muslim community was always microscopically small: 504,000 adherents in 1996 out of a total population of 41 million.[3] About half its members lived in Cape Town; the remainder were almost evenly split between Natal and Transvaal, including clusters of Muslims in the other major port towns—Durban, East London, and Port Elizabeth. Membership included a high percentage of doctors, lawyers, artisans, teachers, and business people, many of them vocal opponents of the apartheid regime, but even more who kept their political opinions to themselves or reserved them for closed-door conversations.

The predictable conflict between traditionalists and innovators in such a setting was a feature of South African Islam, reflected in mosque and media discourse through the 1980s and 1990s. Islam in South Africa was predominantly independent and local, and with more than 450 independent mosques, educational institutions, and social, cultural, or other associations the possibilities for splintering were multiple.[4] Both Sunni and Shiite Islam were represented.

Islam in South Africa established itself in a setting of heavy Christian missionary activity. Three-quarters of South Africans identify themselves as Christians, members of either mainstream denominations or of rapidly spreading independent churches; during the nineteenth century, "the Cape probably was the most heavily missionized area in the world."[5] Islam was attractive to minority South African populations—variously called Malay and later Coloured, as well as Indian—as it later would be for freed slaves. It was a distinctly non-Christian and hence a nonwhite religion; later it would be considered an African religion. This appealed to people subjected to the heavy burdens of Dutch, British, and Afrikaner rule, but some blacks in the late twentieth century would call it an Indian religion, so its appeal was never an unqualified one.

Early History

Islam came to South Africa in three phases, first, during the mid-seventeenth century, when the Dutch East India Company used it as a place to exile recalcitrant Islamic political leaders from its eastern possessions and also imported Muslim slaves to protect its colonial settlement.[6] A century later, in the second wave, nearly 3,000 convicts, mostly from the Indian subcontinent and the Indonesian archipelago, were sent to work on the company's Cape Town harbor and settlement infrastructure. They were followed by a slave population that eventually totaled 63,000 persons (1807), whose numbers included several imams.[7] Since the Dutch forbid open expressions of Islam, worship was held secretly in private homes. As early as 1770, an English explorer observed that some slaves met weekly "in a private house belonging to a free Mohammedan, in order to read, or rather chaunt, several prayers and chapters of the Koran."[8] The third wave came with the formal abolition of slavery in the nineteenth century (1838), when the British established depositories at Cape Town and Sierra Leone where former slaves, called Prize Negroes, were settled. Their numbers included Muslims from elsewhere in Africa.

These three waves of immigration suggest the themes of early South African Islamic history—its members were outsiders and were imported involuntarily from the Indian subcontinent, Indonesia, or elsewhere in Africa. They were also members of a faith community that met secretly. Many were exiled for expounding religious beliefs; still others were religious leaders. Finally, the Islamic presence was shaped in response to two dominant, white, European powers, the Dutch and the British, whose political, military, and educational control over the territory was absolute. Add to that a heavy concentration of zealous Protestant missionaries, and there was not much space in which Islam could easily grow, except within the populations of which it was already a part.

A feature of South African Islam was its innate conservatism. No dominant Islamic political power around which believers could rally ever emerged. Moreover, the core of South African believers were merchants, clerks, and professional people who were not risk-takers by nature. Also, the lack of any organizational structures within the Islamic communities left mosques under the control of individual imams or mosque committees.[9]

Shaykh Yusuf (1626), "Founder" of Islam in South Africa

The first Muslims to enter South Africa were brought there by the Dutch East India Company, anxious to rid its Far East holdings of political-religious dissidents. Possibly this amounted to 200 such persons in the 1652–1795 period.[10] They included a Sufi saint, Shaykh Yusuf, popularly regarded as the founder of Islam in South Africa, although he was not the first Muslim to arrive there. Yusuf, who came from Indonesia in 1626, had made the hajj and married into the family of the king of Goa. He was exiled to South Africa in 1694 at age 68, along with 49 followers. For the next 5 years, his compound, purposefully set by the Dutch far from the main population centers, became a center for Islamic teaching. "These Mohammedans are multiplying rapidly and increasing in numbers,"[11] the Dutch reported in 1699. It is often assumed that Islam grew in South Africa because of increased conversions, but without more thorough research on the subject, it looks as if the growth may simply have been due to the growth of Muslim families.[12]

During the eighteenth century, nearly 3,000 convicts were imported from the Indian subcontinent and Indonesia as manual workers to build the Cape Town harbor and settlement infrastructure. Death rates were high among the transplanted workers, but those who survived were given their freedom; among their numbers were several imams, called Bandit Imams (the Dutch word for "convicts" was *bandietten*).[13] These included several prominent figures, such as Jouddan Tappa Santrij, the Cape's first Muslim martyr, plus other "Mahometaanse priesters," some of whom were chained together. Shell writes, "Such imams represent a spectacular example of colonial status inversion: in settler eyes they were convicts, but in the eyes of the autochthonous, slave, and free black populations they became leaders of an alternative culture."[14] There is a 1725 report of an "elderly Moslem" who was watching Dutch sailors and a prostitute:

> "You Dutch Christians preach to us of your superior religion. The Calvinists are, to hear them, the salt of the earth with God-given morals." Pointing to the line of drunken sailors, he said: 'Look at how you really are. You behave like swine, like drunken, whoring pigs. I would never allow my daughter to marry a Dutchman. I would break her neck first. Now you have the better ships, the bigger guns, and you make us your slaves. But one day Allah will be revenged.' "[15]

Slavery was a feature of company life, and at least 63,000 slaves were landed in South Africa from 1652 to 1807, when the British ended the oceanic slave trade.[16] The slaves were liberated on December 1, 1834, although ex-slaves were retained in effectual bondage as apprentices for an additional 4 years. Possibly half South Africa's slave population came from the Indian subcontinent and the Far East, and another sizable contingent came from Madagascar. Slavery is forbidden in the two sacred books, the Bible and the Koran, but there are examples of leaders of both faiths who owned slaves. There are also instances when Muslims freed both their own slaves and Christian slaves. John Philip, one of the most prominent nineteenth-century Protestant missionaries, observed: "I do not know whether there is a law among the Malays binding them to make their slaves free, but it is known that they seldom retain in slavery those that embrace their religion, and to the honor of the Malays it must be stated many instances have occurred in which, at public sales, they have purchased aged and wretched creatures, irrespective of their religion, to make them free."[17]

Finally, since both Sierra Leone and Cape Town were places where British slave patrols deposited slaves captured on the open seas, 5,000 Prize Negroes, as the Royal Navy called them, were landed at the Cape between 1808 and 1856. Forced into long apprenticeships that differed little from slavery, many became Muslims.[18]

Nineteenth-Century Expansionism

The nineteenth century produced a flowering of Islamic activity and an expansion of local mosques, as the Muslim population of Cape Town increased from 3,000 in 1822 to 11,287 in 1891.[19] Tayob describes life in the Islamic community of this period:

> Blending together Islamic and local religious elements in the Cape, they provided pastoral care during the crucial rites of birth, marriage, illness, and death. Imams officiated at elaborate and colorful naming ceremonies for the newborn (doepmal). They were ready to conduct marriage ceremonies for slaves when Christianity refused them matrimony, and displayed a special concern for the burial of the deceased irrespective of their social positions. Furthermore, the imams taught slave and Free Black children at mosque schools. For most of these children, this was the only kind of education possible.[20]

Activist Sufi mysticism, "dispersed militant mysticism,"[21] as one author has called it, was a feature of South African Islam. Talismans (azimats) were widely used; prayers were addressed at the tombs (karamats) of Sufi saints; and in the face of an oppressive slave regime, Islam provided secret and life-sustaining knowledge, even the power to render a fleeing slave invisible, it was believed.[22] Tuan Guru, an imam brought to the Cape in 1780 and later imprisoned on Robben Island, remarked, "Be of good heart my children and serve your masters; for one day your liberty will be restored to you and your descendants will live within a circle of karamats safe from fire, famine, and plague, earthquake and tidal wave."[23] Later, as the Sufi brotherhoods expanded to include representatives of the Qadiriya, Naqsh-bandi, and Chistiya orders, the tombs of Sufi saints, especially surrounding Cape Town, remained popular sites for local pilgrimages.

Muslims were in demand in nineteenth-century South Africa as workers. As the wine industry grew, they became trusted, nondrinking laborers.

As clerks and artisans, they filled jobs on farms and in businesses, and their reliability brought them opportunities to enter clerical ranks, for which there were never enough European recruits. With the shortage of soldiers, the Cape Muslims enrolled in two Dutch artillery units to fight the British, for which they were rewarded by the right to publicly hold worship services.[24] It is at this time (1798) that the Cape's first mosque was built.

The opening of the Suez Canal in 1869 and the spread of travel by steamship resulted in more people making the hajj; also, Muslims who could afford it were sending their sons to study in Cairo and Mecca, and both groups were returning with an awareness of being part of a wider world of Islam. The English occupation of the Cape in 1795 also brought with it a more permissive religious climate. The number of persons making the hajj increased, and a new Arabic-Afrikaans script was invented, allowing the printing of Islamic sacred literature. Schools were founded, often in association with new mosques, and the Turkish fez was introduced as headgear for men. Petitioned by the Cape Islamic community to provide them with an imam, Queen Victoria sent a Kurdish scholar, Shaykh Abu Bakr Effendi, to the Cape Muslims in 1862 to be their leader, but he never gained local acceptance.[25]

The Arrival of Indian Muslims

Yet another wave of immigrants came to South Africa in the mid-to-late nineteenth century, and with it, the texture of Islam changed. In addition to Cape Town, smaller but strong Islamic communities were now established in Natal and in the Transvaal. More than 176,000 Indian indentured servants arrived in South Africa, principally to work in Natal's sugarcane fields after the British colonization of Natal in the 1860s, and in the diamond mines after 1867; approximately 7% to 10% of them were Muslim.[26] The Natal Muslims came from India and arrived much later than the Cape Muslims. Once they completed their time as indentured servants, many Natal Muslims moved inland for jobs with the growing mining industry during the 1867–1948 period.

A number of skilled Indian traders were also drawn to Natal and formed perhaps 10% of its Muslim community. Natal Islam contained many vestiges of traditional Indian religion, but organizationally the influence of the pragmatic traders through mosque committees was heavy; thus, differences among mosques were less visibly pronounced than in the Cape. Among the Natal Muslims, a leading presence was Shaykh Ahmas, reputedly a Sufi miracle worker, who also worked as a Durban fruit dealer until his death in 1886. An equally important figure was Shah Ghulum Muhhad Soofie Siddiqui, who created several schools, orphanages, and special Islamic folk festivals with processions, music, and cultural programs after his arrival in 1895.[27]

Differences Within South African Islam

Clear differences separated Cape and Natal Muslims. Cape Muslims were largely Afrikaans or creole Dutch speakers, and artisans and workers led their congregations; Natal Indian Muslims were led primarily by merchants who were speakers of Urdu, Tamil, English, and other Indian languages.[28] Internal migrations resulted in the emergence of a third regional Muslim community in the Transvaal. Johannesburg, in the early twentieth century, was South Africa's most modern city, and both Hanafi and Shafii Muslims were attracted to it.[29]

In 1903 a Transvaal Muslim, al-Hajj Mustafa al-Transvaal, submitted three questions to the grand mufti of Egypt, seeking an authoritative legal interpretation (fatwa) on issues faced by modernizing Islamic societies. Could Muslims wear European hats while conducting trade? Could they eat meat slaughtered by Christian butchers, who did not say the Bishmallah before killing the animals? And could an imam trained in one school (Hanafi) lead followers of another legal school (Shafi) in worship? Muhammad Abduh, a well-respected Egyptian jurist, produced a liberal and inclusive response, which provoked controversy throughout the Muslim world, as the answers might today. His basic position was that Muslim unity was more important than arguing over minute details of ritual observance. Voll has called the finding "one of the famous documents of early Islamic modernist thought."[30] For South African Islam, it was an opportunity to engage in dialogue with respected overseas sources on important legal and theological questions, a discourse that has continued throughout the history of Islam in South Africa.

The proliferation of mosques in the mid-nineteenth century resulted in rivalries among imams and their followers, and disputes over rituals and teachings were a feature of local Islamic life. The question of succession to mosque leadership was always touchy since Islam had no ordained clerical class. However, successful imams were anxious to pass on their positions to their sons, some of whom were considerably less skilled and pious than their fathers. At least 20 mosque leadership disputes found their way to the Cape Supreme Court between 1866 and 1900.[31]

The 1886 Cemetery Uprising

A pivotal event in the life of the Cape Town Islamic community was the 1886 cemetery uprising. When the colonial authorities closed traditional Muslim burial places for health reasons after a smallpox epidemic, the Islamic community protested and then revolted when local administrators refused to listen to them. Muslims objected to their bodies being pierced by needles; their sick being moved from homes to hospitals, where food preparation would not observe Halaal standards; and their dead being buried in cemeteries that could not be reached by mourners who were carrying the body of the deceased. A protest demonstration of over 3,000 people took place at the burial of a child, and the demonstrators were arrested. The cemetery uprisings were a galvanic event in the life of the wider Islamic community, registering its protests to the powerful colonial figures over central religious issues, involving health and the ritual burial of the dead.[32]

Islam in the Era of Apartheid (1948–1994)

Islam as it emerged in South Africa split along lines experienced elsewhere; in short, it was a classic ancients versus moderns division—traditionalists who argued that the only answers came from the words and experience of the Prophet and his times, and those who respected the Koran but thought it was compatible with an adaptable approach to the issues of modern society. The conflict was summarized in the lives of two brothers-in-law, Abdullah Abduhuraman (1872–1940), a Glasgow-trained physician and well-known exponent of secular and religious education, and Shaykh Muhammad Salieh Hendricks (1871–1945), a conservative who sought to isolate Muslim women from modern influences.[33] Abduhuraman founded a number of Muslim mission schools, providing a better standard of education for young Muslims while shielding them from Christian schools, which would undermine Islamic teachings.

A Muslim Judicial Council (MJC) was founded in Cape Town in 1945 to both define Islamic customs and represent the Muslim community to the state. Drawing membership from approximately 100 mosques in the Cape region, it adjudicated civil disputes among Muslims. Dominated by older religious leaders, the MJC was criticized as being too conservative and lacking in power. In the 1980s, the organization was wracked by financial scandals and ideological disputes between reformers and radicals. A comparable group, the Natal Jamiat al-Ulama (Council of Theologians) was created in 1952. Its membership was often involved in sharp sectarian quarrels with other Muslim groups. Originally a group of heterogeneous religious scholars, it later was made up largely of Deobandi-inclined teachers. The name Deobandi comes from the location in India of an Islamic seminary established in colonial times. Deobandi followers tend to practice a puritanical form of personal Islamic practice while leaving politics to the wary traders who run the mosque committees.[34]

In October 1986, the Muslim community united briefly to condemn a Dutch Reformed Synod resolution—offered at a church synod by the chaplain-general of the South African police—that branded Islam as a "false religion" and "a threat to the world." Representing the Muslim Youth Movement, Muhammed Farid voiced a sentiment echoed by other Muslim groups when he demanded an apology from the Dutch Reformed Church, the white Afrikaans establishment church, and President Pieter Botha. An inflammatory, detailed "explanation" by the church only hardened the historic divisions.[35]

The history of Islam in South Africa is dotted with a number of small organizations designed to advance Muslim political, professional, and community interests. Compared to Islamic groups in some other African states, the South African organizations would be considered small, but they are generally well organized, some of them with cells—as would be the case with revolutionary groups in an authoritarian setting. Also, many of the groups keenly follow global political-religious issues. The first such group to assume political coloration was the Muslim Teachers' Association (1951), which objected to Muslims being categorized as Malay under the Population Registration Act and to community participation in the annual Voortrekker celebration, commemorating the Afrikaners' occupation of the interior.[36]

Other significant modern groups, usually small but focused on their interests, include the Call of Islam, the largest radical Muslim group in South Africa, with numerous small cells. Founded in 1984 in Cape Town, it is capable of gathering thousands of demonstrators for rallies. The Muslim Student Association, first organized in Cape Town in 1980, has wide support on university campuses. Its several hundred members actively organized anti–United States and anti-Israeli demonstrations during the Gulf war. A Muslim Lawyers' Association supports making Muslim personal law, a modified version of Sharia, acceptable in South Africa. A Muslim Meat Traders' Association, a conservative group, condemned the U.S. presence in the Persian Gulf. The Islamic Medical Association, made up of a thousand medical doctors and health workers, supported striking hospital workers in Natal in 1992.[37] An Islamic Propagation Centre in

Durban, and the Islamic Missionary Society, the Central Islamic Trust, and the Muslim Dawah Society, all in Johannesburg, carry out missionary activities.

Islam has also expanded elsewhere in South Africa and may have attracted 2,000 whites and 20,000 blacks by century's end. The Soweto Muslim Association, which opened a mosque in 1986, claims 5,000 members. A Muslim Community Association, founded in 1985 by university students in Cape Province, proselytizes in black townships, as does the more radical Islamic Movement of Kwa-Zulu and Natal.

Imam Abdullah Haron

Imam Abdullah Haron went about the countryside of the Western Cape as a salesman of Rowntree-Wilson chocolates, but he ended his life in a South African prison, dying on September 29, 1969, after "falling down stairs" in prison, as the police claimed. He emerged as one of the country's leading martyrs, a figure comparable to Steve Biko, who perished in similar brutal circumstances in 1977. It was Imam Haron, head of the Al Jaamia Mosque in the Claremont suburb of Cape Town since 1956, who symbolized Muslim opposition to apartheid and drew an increasingly large group of younger people as followers, for which he paid with his life.[38]

Gregarious and athletic, a swimmer and rugby and cricket player, he was the successful leader of his own mosque and the founder of others. Haron had been to Mecca three times, thanks to the generosity of an aunt, and was fluent in Arabic. His wife, Galiema, was an expert seamstress, as well as the mother of their three children.

An immediate problem facing Haron and his congregation—and all nonwhites—was the devastating effects of the Group Areas Act, by which black and colored communities could be summarily evicted from ancestral or long-held lands. Haron gained notoriety when he led the Muslim community in protest of the removal of mosques, causing their exemption from the Group Areas Act, one of the few successful acts of opposition to that law.[39] Haron was a constant voice on such political issues, condemning the Bantu Education, Coloured Education, and Group Areas Acts of 1961. The last, he said, "is designed to cripple us educationally, politically, and economically."[40]

Haron was active in converting urban, black Africans to Islam. Disgusted with what they had experienced of white, Christian civilization, many found in Islam a more acceptable, more African religion. An editor of *Muslim News*[41] and member of the outlawed Coloured People's Congress, he traveled to Mecca, Cairo, and Amsterdam, where he spoke out against apartheid. Haron allowed young believers to preside over birth, marriage, and funeral ceremonies and to give the Friday lecture at his mosque.[42] By sharing power with the young laity and by criticizing the failure of traditional leaders to distribute alms (zakat) to the needy, the Muslim leader eventually brought opprobrium upon established shaykhs and imams, anxious to preserve their theological, financial, and liturgical turf, and upon the Muslim Judicial Council, even though he was a member. Founded in 1958, his Claremont Muslim Youth Association (CMYA) was an activist, antiapartheid counterpart to the MJC, providing material assistance to political detainees and vocally protesting apartheid policies to the international press. On May 7, 1961, the CMYA organized a broad-based meeting of 4,000 Muslims at the Cape Town Drill Hall to demonstrate apartheid's contradictions with Islamic teachings on justice and equity. An account of the meeting said in part:

> For too long now have we been together with our fellow-sufferers, subjugated, humiliated of being regarded as inferior beings, deprived of our basic rights to earn, to learn and to worship freely to the Divine Rule of Allah.
> By proclamations under the Group Areas Act we are deprived of our homes and places of worship. Even if our sacred mosques are not removed the fact [is] that we will be driven out of our settled homes, an act of tyranny, a transgression of our fundamental rights which no true Muslim should allow to pass.[43]

Haron was arrested on May 28, 1969, the birthday of the Prophet, and held without charges for 5 months. He was found dead in his cell on May 27, 1969. Police said he died from a fall downstairs, although an autopsy disclosed multiple beatings; local and international efforts to ascertain what exactly happened and who was responsible for his death were met with official stonewalling.[44]

The popular leader's death left South African Muslims with a dilemma. Should the response be to head for the mosque and pray or to turn into the streets and demonstrate? Both positions had their followers and detractors, and the issue was never settled. How could it be? Conservative professionals were apt to internalize their opposition to apartheid and not go public about it, for there was always the omnipresent state security apparatus, infiltrating every organization, using paid or coerced informers, and reminding potential opponents of the price they would pay, from job loss to torture. Even the spirited CMYA had been pressured to curb its activities and become the Ibadur-Rahman Study Group.[45] Still, Islamic antiapartheid activists continued, often in consort with their Christian counterparts, but the basic conservative-activist divide continued as an enduring feature of South African Islam.

A Divided Community

Meanwhile, Cape-Natal and Cape-Transvaal differences remained as pronounced as ever. In Natal, the Indian Islamic community placed a high priority on education and, through the Natal Muslim Council, became the voice of the Indian desire to integrate Muslim values and modern education, including education for women. Aware of the low standard of Islamic education in the province, the council sought to improve the quality of both religious and government schools.[46] Finding the teachers wanting—they had migrated from the villages of India—the council contributed funds for an institute of higher Islamic studies, which it hoped would raise up local instructors "qualified in religion, modern technique and modern education."[47]

Natal Muslims were also split between those who argued that Arabic must be introduced as the fundamental language of Islamic education and an equally vociferous element that urged that Urdu, widely used in schools and mosques, be retained as the lingua franca. The Arabic Study Circle brought speakers to the region, encouraged debates, and offered scholarships for study abroad. The Natal Muslims remained basically more conservative than their Cape Town counterparts and retained an essentially educational and welfare focus, cautiously negotiating with the state whenever possible for favorable policy changes and funds.

In the Transvaal, access to schools was no less an issue, one that was never satisfactorily resolved for resources were meager and the community was divided between modernists and groups like the Jamiatul Ulama Transvaal, which sought to control Islamic education. "The weakness of Islamic resurgence in the Transvaal is very clear. It seems that during the 1950s, faint signs of Islamic resurgence were beginning to appear. However, in the absence of modern Muslim schools and the rising power of the Jamiatul Ulama Transvaal, support for an alternative understanding of Islam remained isolated."[48]

Muslim interest in promoting education was understandable. Mission schools taught the Christian religion, which was unacceptable to Muslims, and the quality of instruction in government schools was abysmally low. In 1950, only 362 children passed matriculation tests out of 200,000 who started the program 12 years earlier. As late as 1988, the teacher-pupil ratio was 1 to 44.[49]

The Muslim Youth Movement

The Muslim Youth Movement (MYM) was founded in Durban in December 1970 and soon became a national organization, calling the attention of young people to Islam as a way of life and confronting the South African government directly on apartheid. Its rise in the 1970s coincided with that of the Black Consciousness Movement, with which it was closely allied. Both groups strongly opposed Western influences, and they made some effort to attract black members through programs to distribute blankets and food parcels in black townships and to "invite a brother of African origin for a meal," but not much came of the effort.[50] The goals of the MYM remained largely change through education, as possibilities of revolutionary armed conflict were impossible in the South African police state.[51]

The MYM met opposition from the conservative Muslim Judicial Council and with Islamist groups like the Deobandis, which wanted no tampering with their perceived understanding of Islam as a religious, not a political, force. By 1958 the number of MYM branches had risen to 31, all of them promoting Koranic studies and other educational activities. The Women's Council was organized in Durban in 1972 so that women could attend Ramadan prayers. One of the group's guiding principles was to "make Muslim women an integral part of the whole program," but this meant only a parallel program for women, and it failed to attract a following.[52] The place of women in Islamic life was hotly debated. The MYM wanted women to attend prayer services at mosques on Fridays and special days, but the Muslim majority opposed such a practice, arguing that the Prophet intended women to pray at home. The added argument was that Umar I, the second caliph of Islam, had banned women from mosques because he feared that male worshippers would be sexually distracted.[53]

Given the range of viewpoints represented in South African Islam, competition among its religious leaders, and the geographic isolation of its components into three major centers, it is a wonder that the MYM achieved all that it did. It became the first national Muslim movement in South Africa, and it attempted to raise the country's Islamic educational standards. At the same time, it confronted sensitive issues, such as responses to apartheid, the place of women, the type of education to be offered, contacts with the wider world of Islam in the Middle East and elsewhere, and opening Islam to membership from the black townships. The MYM deserves credit for being a focal point for virtually all of the political, educational, and social issues facing contemporary Islam in South Africa.

Islam in the New Century: Religion in an Emerging Society

Under apartheid, the South African Muslim community represented a minority within a minority, with economic power out of proportion to its numbers and with many of its members being well educated, politically conservative, living in urban areas, and holding skilled or semiskilled jobs.[54]

Some South African Muslims were represented in the Islamic Council of South Africa (ICSA), established in 1975 and quartered in the Indian business section of Durban. Funded by the Saudi government, the ICSA was a tolerant, nonmilitant clearinghouse, representing Muslim interests. As such, it satisfied neither Islamists nor more conservative groups. The Juma Musjid Trust, which controlled Durban's Grey Street Mosque, the largest in the southern hemisphere, quit the ICSA in 1983 because the organization opposed the government's constitutional proposals. The Sydenham Muslim Association also left the ICSA, saying it had no mandate to engage in political activities.[55]

For most South African Muslims, moderation and political fence sitting were a way of life in the 1980s. Little would be gained, in their view, if a black government replaced a white one. Increasingly, as the prospect of independence became a reality, this viewpoint changed. Muslims began to voice opposition to apartheid and find a place within the African National Congress (ANC). Muslim proselytizers became active in black African communities, and more militant groups, peopled by younger Muslims, redefined the parameters of discourse. For many, the 1979 Iranian revolution was a defining moment: an Islamic government could seize power against seemingly impossible odds in a police state, thus sounding the first trumpets of a global Islamic revolution. Other, more conservative Muslims, such as the leadership of the ICSA, viewed the Ayatollah Khomeini as a reactionary, antimodern figure, and most South African Muslims realized that the Iranian revolution was led by the mullahs, and South Africa's imams were far from being revolutionaries.

Also during the 1980s, a growing Islamic consciousness, a counterpart of black consciousness, became a feature of South Africa. It included efforts to improve Muslim education, increase charitable work at home and abroad, and promote departments of Islamic studies in South African universities. Several thousand South African Muslims made the hajj to Mecca each year, bringing them in contact with the wider world of Islam as an international presence.

The moderate orientation of most South African Muslims was reflected in the debate over Salman Rushdie's *The Satanic Verses*. Disagreeing with the Ayatollah Khomeini's call for the author's assassination and the offer of $1 million to carry out the deed, the Call of Islam and Muslim Youth League condemned the novel but distanced their organizations from the assassination order. "Islamic tenets and ethics demand due process of law take place. . . . Rushdie should give substance to his apology by removing those provocative and offensive portions of his novel."[56]

The Muslim Front was cobbled together in 1990, and it actively supported the militant ANC in 1994. Since independence that year, some Muslims joined two small parties, the African Muslim Party and the Islamic Party, but neither gained any seats in Parliament. Muslims attached themselves where they could, primarily as individuals or representatives of small factions, since no united Muslim political voice was ever a reality. "You will hardly find a mosque in South Africa that is not aflame with conflict and controversy, sometimes ending in physical violence," the head of the South African Islamic Council, Muhammad Shir Shawdhari remarked, adding that many religious leaders who immigrated from India, Pakistan, and Bangladesh split the South African Islamic community by their own divisions. "These people, who call themselves 'scholars' (ulma), accept no discussion or debate."[57]

Notwithstanding the difficulties and despite their small numbers, an articulate Islamic presence was a feature of modern South African life. The successful ANC named a respected Muslim jurist, Abdullah Omar, as minister of justice in a national unity government. (In August 1996, Omar moved out of his residence in the troubled Cape Flats, where his home had been sacked by Islamist radicals.) Judge Ismail Mahomed, a senior civil and criminal litigation lawyer and human rights activist, was named the first post-Apartheid chief justice. As such, he became head of the country's highest court of appeals.[58] A feature of South African Islam was its high level of interest in wider Islamic issues, from the Gulf war to the situation of Muslims in the Balkans and from news of Muslims in Malaysia to the growing presence of Muslims in the United States.

In the fragmented society of century's-end South Africa, several contradictory indications of Muslim interests were manifest. A Jewish bookstore owner was attacked in 1997 on the eve of Cape Town's bid for the Olympic Games, and a mosque in Rustenberg was bombed. Some Muslims reasserted their "Malay" identity in 1994 as the government reached a trade and cultural exchange agreement with Malaysia.[59] In August 1998, the Jamiatul Ulama of Kwazulu-Nata issued a statement decrying the August 25, 1998, bombing of the Planet Hollywood restaurant at the Waterfront, Cape Town, as an "act of terror by faceless and cowardly perpetrators to keep communities at ransom."[60]

In short, a legacy of violence was part of South African history. Rule of law was never available to the disenfranchised, and the instruments of state were designed to suppress open civic participation. On March 21, 1960, inexperienced white police officers fired on African demonstrators at the Sharpsville Police Station, killing 69 persons, including women and children, and wounding 180. By the mid-1980s, over half the deaths in some urban areas were from homicides, and many inhabitants of crowded, drug- and alcohol-ridden townships could subscribe to the fatalistic motto of young Sophiatown *totsis* (gangsters): "Live well, die young, and leave a good-looking corpse."[61]

The Iranian revolution was a signal event for many South African Muslims, and when the Gulf war broke out, Muslims were quick to protest American and Israeli activities. Likewise, American missile attacks in the Sudan and in Afghanistan brought widespread petitions and protests. On October 10, 1997, Muslims gathered in Pretoria to decry Israeli atrocities against Palestinians, carrying posters with slogans like "One bullet, one Zionist." In such a political setting, young South African Muslims came of age.

The South African Muslim response to the September 11, 2001, terrorist attacks in America was mixed. Generally, the loss of innocent civilian lives was regretted, although People Against Gangsterism and Drugs (PAGAD) declined to make any public statement.[62] The conservative Durban *Jamiatul Ulama* wrote, "It is indeed a great pity that ordinary civilians become victims of political deception and duplicity. They are the innocent pawns who pay the price of embargos, sanctions, murder, and pillage on behalf of their political masters."[63] The article warned that the attacks will create an identity crisis for Muslims: "We must guard against falling prey to internal conflict within the Ummah, by debating the integrity of the Taliban, by questioning the legitimacy of their rule; this is not the time for Muslim discord and bickering."[64]

Terrorism Linked to Islam

PAGAD

The collapse of public order in postindependence South Africa remained a concern of all parties. More than 200 bombing incidents have been recorded since 1996.[65] In 1996 an Islamic-related organization called People against Gangsterism and Drugs was formed, drawing its core membership from working-class Muslims from the Cape Flats section of Cape Town. One press report described it as "a Muslim fundamentalist organization committed to opposing the liberal democratic state."[66] Its members dressed like Middle Eastern Muslims, and took the law into their own hands as a way of confronting drug dealers.[67] Such activity was not uncommon; during the apartheid era, "peoples' courts," distrustful of the white-led judicial system, carried out their own sentencing, including beatings and executions. Since independence, an understaffed, ineffectual, and often corrupt police force has been unable to provide protection against a rising crime rate. Sheikh Sa'dullah Khan, director of the Gatesville Islamic Center in a section from which many PAGAD members come, observed that people of the Cape Flats "feel they've asked the police [to stop crime] and the police haven't done it, so now they will do it."[68]

Whatever its original intentions, PAGAD was soon linked with drive-by shootings and pipe bombings, some of them triggered by remote control, and armed shootings with gangsters. Its shift to increasing criminal action caused PAGAD to lose support within the South African Muslim community and to become a target for police of the newly independent state. A judge was killed, as was a witness in a criminal trial against a PAGAD member. Allegedly, PAGAD plotted to kill magistrates "who wanted to sentence a member of the Muslim community or a PAGAD member."[69] Using a veneer of Islamic language, PAGAD became another armed vigilante group.

The ability of PAGAD to muster large crowds of antidrug demonstrators waned significantly since the mainline Muslim Judicial Council denounced its antistate and anti–Muslim establishment activities in January 1997. Since November 1998, 16 PAGAD members were convicted of crimes and 14 were acquitted. A hundred cases were pending against organization members, including murder and attempted murder cases.[70] The U.S. State Department listed PAGAD as a terrorist organization; moreover, in response to its activities and a declining climate of public safety, the South African government proposed an antiterrorism bill that allowed police to hold suspects 14 days without bail, the kind of measure that was common in the apartheid era. The United Ulama Council of South Africa protested the draft bill on September 18, 2000, saying it would violate due process of law and "the right to be presumed innocent."[71]

Qiblah

An even more extreme group was Qiblah, which the minister of justice linked with PAGAD as a terrorist organization. (Both PAGAD and Qiblah were among the 43 groups on the U.S. State Department's international terrorist list.) Qiblah, founded in Cape Town in 1977 by dissidents from the Muslim Students Association, was named for the mosque niche that always points toward Mecca. Organized in small cells similar to revolutionary groups elsewhere, it attracted young intellectuals and professionals and drew membership from the Cape colored community. It espoused an Iranian-Khomeini model of Islamic fundamentalist ideology. Its leader, Achmat Cassiem, was jailed for advocating antistate views, and he spent 1964–1969 on Robben Island. During Ramadan 1990, Qiblah called for creation of an Islamic state and for Muslims to engage in combat and prepare for a jihad.[72] Qiblah reportedly received money from the Palestine Liberation Organization, trained assassins in Libya, and welcomed Islamist terrorists arriving in or traveling through South Africa.[73] In the post September 11, 2001, period it urged South African Muslims to fight a jihad in Afghanistan against the United States. Muslims against Illegitimate Leaders, a small organization in the Western Cape claims to have recruited a thousand volunteers to fight in Afghanistan. In contrast, the South African Ministry of Foreign Affairs said that anyone who went to fight in Afghanistan would be arrested on his return.[74] In a rare public interview, Cassiem, his remarks dipped in bitterness, justified violence:

> The retaliation by the oppressed people is always justified in view of the fact of what the oppressor is doing. . . . I was born and bred in South Africa. I lived in a terrorist state since the time of my birth and I fought the terrorist state with everything at my disposal because I don't believe that any human being can be moderate in demanding what is rightfully theirs. So when it comes to a question of being an extremist you have to see in perspective what exactly you are extreme about.[75]

Muslim Personal Law

The Sharia issue, a source of confrontation all over Africa, was equally contentious in South Africa but in a different context than elsewhere. South African Muslims did not ask for adoption of the whole Sharia, a political impossibility, but argued for the acceptance of parts of it, principally those sections dealing with family law, custody, and inheritance. They accepted the South African constitutionalists' argument that customary or traditional law should not conflict with wider, international norms of human and gender rights. In short, progressives saw the Sharia injunctions as parts of a whole. "To isolate the rules from their context and argue for their artificial transplantation into a non-Islamic society is to reduce an entire world view to a set of punishments," the Call of Islam, the country's largest radical Muslim organization, argued in 1994 in a pamphlet entitled "Must Muslims Vote for a Muslim Party?"[76] Clearly the Bill of Rights provisions of the October 1996 South African Constitution conflicted with those of the Sharia, especially sections of the postapartheid Constitution that gave all persons equal protection under the law and prohibited direct or indirect discrimination against anyone on grounds of "race, gender, pregnancy, marital status, ethnic or social origin, color, sexual orientation, age, disability, religion, conscience, belief, culture, language and birth." Progressive Muslims argued the compatibility of both legal systems, a solution that if adopted elsewhere in Africa would break the impasse in which many states find themselves. But such a position would never satisfy Islamists, who held to an inclusive, traditional Sharia until the end, arguing that to do otherwise is to forsake Islam's basic beliefs.

In South Africa, Muslim marriages have never been legal, and as late as 1998 their status was unclear. "The current position however is that South African civil law and MPL [Muslim personal law] exist in mutual disregard of each other," Mahomed and Moosa write, adding, "Until change occurs (i.e. in terms of legal, structural and institutional reform), the status quo poses significant problems and challenges for Muslim South Africans and the institutions that regulate MPL seeking the protection and promotion of their rights under the rule of law."[77] The issue was exacerbated by a court case, *Amod v. the Multilateral Motor Vehicle Accidents Fund*, in which a Durban court dismissed a Muslim widow's claim for compensation for loss of support because, under law, no legal marriage existed. The case was appealed and decided in favor of the widow. The state of MPL in South Africa remains in a legislative limbo, although courts began to recognize the legal standing of Muslim marriage contracts without endorsing the validity of the marriages. Meanwhile, sharp divisions remained among Muslims over the issue of making Muslim family law compatible with the South African constitution.[78]

Gender Issues: Women in the Mosque

The role of women has been hotly debated in South Africa's Muslim communities. The viewpoint of traditionalists is well known, but in South Africa some of the continent's most progressive Islamic sentiment in support of women has been voiced, positions that if enacted would give Muslim women the status dictated by international human rights accords.

Womens' issues were in the national forefront when the independent station Radio Islam excluded women's voices from the air, arguing that the voice was part of a woman's body that must be concealed. Moreover, the sounds of a woman's voice could tempt male listeners, station owners believed. A complaint against the station was brought by a Muslim youth group in Johannesburg.[79] The case was appealed to the country's Independent Broadcasting Authority, supported by both the Muslim Youth Movement and the Commission on Gender Equality. Using provisions of the Bill of Rights as a norm, the commission found in favor of the petitioners, and the station, which claimed to be the only authentic voice for Islam in the world, lost its broadcast license.[80]

A historic event occurred when a woman, Professor Amina Wadud Muhsin of the Commonwealth University of Virginia, was allowed to deliver a presermon lecture from the main floor of the mosque on Friday, August 11, 1994, at the Claremont Main Road Mosque, a progressive institution. Esack described the event:

> While several women had, in fact, previously addressed men in mosques in South Africa, this was the first time that it was on the occasion of the congregational prayers on a Friday. Although it preceded the more formal ritual of a rehearsed Arabic sermon, in the religious *imaginaire* of Muslims it was every bit as significant as the sermon itself. The mosque was packed and the mood, rather than curious, was euphoric and celebratory. The women, many clad in black with only their faces and hands exposed, had until that day usually worshipped upstairs. Now they came down, sat in space normally reserved for men, separated by a piece of rope, and never went back again.[81]

Conclusions: Bourgeois Islam, Radicalism, and Political Uncertainty

The main conclusions about the present and future of Islam in South Africa are as follows:

- Islam's numbers are among the lowest of any country in Africa, and Islam will remain a distinctly minority religion.
- Geographical separation and the personalities of the numerous individual imams around which mosques and their congregations gravitate make it difficult to obtain a unified perspective and make common cause on any given issue.
- The place of women may be marginally better in South Africa than elsewhere in Africa, at least in progressive Islamic circles. A range of modern women's issues has been raised, including equal participation in mosque services and in delivering the Friday message; a place for women in the deliberations of the mosque communities; and questions of dress, employment, divorce, and property and inheritance rights.
- The historic split between ancients and moderns, conservatives and progressives, remains undiminished. A strong element of conservative "bourgeois Islam," reflecting the outlook of established professionals and artisans, is a feature of South African life.
- Also a feature of South African life is a small strain of violent radical activists, blurring the boundaries of criminal activity and religious belief. Such groups look to North African and Middle Eastern terrorist groups for support.
- Conversely, South African Muslims include some of Islam's most articulate international voices, figures like Farid Esack, Abdulkader Tayob, and Ebrahim Moosa. Within the progressive wing of Islamic thought, they have bridged the gap between an isolated minority movement and a worldwide audience, including global interfaith listeners.
- Ultimately, the advancement of Islam is only possible in relation to the stability of South African society, and at this point maintaining public order is a major challenge.

Conclusion

"If you want to talk to the head of Islam in Africa, whom do you call?" The question is a logical one after the September 11, 2001, terrorist attacks. The answer is that numerous phone calls would be needed throughout the continent, along with letters, emails, faxes, and Internet contacts with several thousand imams and brotherhood leaders representing a bewildering range of traditions and viewpoints, from conservative and mystical to violent and revolutionary.

The five countries selected for this book represent the diversity of traditions and identities of Africa's 150 million to 160 million Muslims. In Nigeria, large Muslim populations go head to head with equally sizable Christian populations, often in violent confrontations over the issue of introducing the Sharia in an ethnically plural, federalist state.

In Sudan, a buffer state between North and sub-Saharan Africa, one of the world's most enduring civil wars is the backdrop of acrimonious conflicts between a Muslim North and a Christian South, both with significant internal divisions of their own.

In Senegal, one of Africa's most stable states, a large Muslim population, primarily made up of members of two prominent brotherhoods, provides a dominant political-religious presence but faces the challenges of aging leadership, depleted environmental resources, and poor economic prospects.

In Kenya, coastal, urbanized "Arab" minorities attracted by secessionist options combine with an equally marginalized Somali Muslim population, producing a sizable minority that is resentful of blatant "Christian" political control in Nairobi.

In South Africa, a small (less than 2% of the population) Islamic population reflects sharp ethnic and ideological divisions while caught between majority white and black populations, all trying to establish themselves in the harsh aftermath of apartheid.

Popular Islam, a Distorted Image

This book suggests, as does recent American and Western encounters with the world of Islam, that it is not enough to consider the complex histories and theologies represented by Muslims across Africa with the views of an earlier era—the time of pith helmets and colonial maps—or of cold war politics. Recent anthropological literature has taught what skilled historians have always known, that the observer's point of view must not be so reflective of the writer's own culture as to distort the reality of the subject being considered. The special need for clarity of vision is underscored in a recent study of how Muslims are portrayed in American films. Jack G. Shaheen's survey of over 900 films concludes that the popular image of Arabs is a sharply distorted one, of shifty, oleaginous characters following a strange god. This is the world of Islam in films like *Tarzan's Revenge* (1928) and *Rules of Engagement* (2000).[1] Similar depictions are not far behind in other media such as the assumptions of many writers on foreign affairs; the description of Islam in Samuel Huntington's "The Clash of Civilizations?" is only one example.[2]

Similarly, the post–September 11, 2001, events have produced a range of surprising (to outsiders) reactions from African Muslims. Most expressed sympathy for the loss of lives in New York and Washington, but some are quick to add a message to the effect that "now you know what it is like to suffer" or "America's tight relationship with Israel brought this on." Kenyans demonstrated in the streets following Friday prayers at a large Nairobi mosque, chanting pro–Osama bin Laben slogans. In South Africa, an extremist group claimed it could muster a thousand young men to fight in Afghanistan. Faced with such a perplexing range of anti-Western responses, an obvious question is this: how could African Muslims hold such a distorted view of the West, and of America in particular?

The intent of this book is not to provide instant political analysis but to trace the unique histories of Islamic communities in Africa and the clashes and evolutions that made them emerge differently, for better or for worse, in modern nation-states. Out of such a cauldron comes the identity of a people. For African Muslims, it includes an awareness of being part of a religion that offers both a moral code for daily living and the promise of a better life in the world to come. Such a belief system makes a believer part of a global community (*umma*) in ways citizenship in a nation-state can never duplicate. Likewise Islamic identity is strengthened in relationship to those outside its accepted circle by crafting a world of instant enemies—of infidels, heretics, and the ignorant (*jahiliyya*).

Islamists

Any study of Islam in Africa must consider the place of fundamentalists (Islamists) in that continent's growing Islamic community. The danger is that given Africa's porous borders, such groups can move about freely, using local Islamic communities as bases from which to launch their destructive activity. This is what happened in Kenya and Tanzania in 1998 when the American embassies were bombed. And in South Africa, groups like PAGAD and Qiblah provide a welcome haven for Middle Eastern extremist groups on their way to somewhere else. Given the easy access of such groups to modern weapons and communications technologies and the relative lack of resources of African police agencies, African targets could be fair game for extremists.

Often more political than theological in their aspirations, this small but vocal and potentially violent community generally pushes for adoption of the Sharia as a country's legal system (although some, like Nigeria's Zak Zaky, argue that the country is not ready for Sharia). Other goals include an end to corruption and a more equitable distribution of economic resources, as well as political reforms, sometimes with the call for a "just ruler" to transform society in ways presidents and generals have not. Finally, there is a widespread condemnation of loose morals, presumably caused by the West, along with an eager embracing of state-of-the-art Western technologies to disseminate the Islamist message. Usually there is also a nostalgic appeal to a golden age that never was.

There is no certainty that the Islamist position will advance in Africa, although its adherents can always be destructive while shielding and supporting terrorists. Opposing the Islamists are the central governments, often led by Muslims or with Muslims in key positions; traditional rulers; and Sufi and other brotherhood clerics and imams with more moderate outlooks and vested political-economic interests. Muslim communities will grow rapidly in Africa—their growth may be due as much to growing birthrates as to conversions—but the fissiparous nature of such loosely organized religious bodies will continue to leave them divided and with diminished political influence. Most likely the future will see no abatement of violence, especially the violence associated with intra-Muslim competition and with Christian-Muslim friction. Such competition will dissipate resources that could be aimed at other pressing developmental needs unless there is some yet unforetold movement for the two peoples of the Book to work together toward peace and reconciliation. It will be a difficult but not impossible road, and there is no alternative, except chaos and violence.

The West should not be discouraged. Opportunities for positive engagement with Africa's Muslim communities and states abound on the political, social, religious, economic, and cultural level. Most African Muslims are moderate in outlook, seeing a more just world: honest, efficient, and responsive government; jobs for their members; and educational opportunities for their children. It is the ancient role of the diplomat, business representative, and student of other cultures to find a reasonable avenue of exploration and accommodation with countries and cultures that differ from our own.

Notes

Acknowledgments

1. Quoted in Harrow, "Islamic Literature in Africa," p. 526.

Introduction

1. Wall, "Reel Bad Arabs," p. 37; Shaheen, *Reel Bad Arabs*.
2. Von Sievers, "Patterns of Islamization and Varieties of Religious Experience Among Muslims of Africa," p. 33.
3. Maalouf, *Crusades Through Arab Eyes*, pp. 265–266.
4. Voll, "Islam in Africa."
5. Quoted in Bravmann, "Islamic Art and Material Culture in Africa," p. 511.
6. Ali, "Islamism," p. 25.
7. Manger, *Muslim Diversity*, p. 4.
8. Quoted in Hunwick, "Sub-Saharan Africa and the Wider World of Islam," p. 28.
9. Ibid., p. 29.
10. Voll, "Islam as a Special World System," p. 222.
11. Adas, *Islamic and European Expansion*.
12. Levtzion, "Islam in the Bilad al-Sudan," pp. 63–93.
13. L'African, *Description de L'Afrique*.
14. Shell, "Islam in Southern Africa," p. 327.
15. Ali, "Islamism," p. 25.
16. Loimeier, *Islamic Reform and Political Change in Northern Nigeria*, p. 17.
17. Von Sievers, "Patterns of Islamization," p. 33.

Chapter 1

1. In delivering the blows, the agent who wields the cane must hold the Koran under his arm so that in effect he swings only from the elbow, which significantly reduces the damage done by the blows. Personal communication, Mitchell Moss, Abuja, Nigeria, April 19, 2000.

2. *Guardian*, March 30, 2000.

3. *Sunday Tribune*, April 2, 2000.

4. *Post Express*, April 27, 2000.

5. *Vanguard*, May 1, 2000; *Post Express*, April 27, 2000.

6. Mukhtari Shitu, oral interview, Abuja, Nigeria, March 28, 2000.

7. *Post Express*, April 27, 2000.

8. *New Nigerian*, May 1, 2000.

9. Ibn Battuta, quoted in "Corpus, 302," in Levtzion and Pouwels. p. 80.

10. Paden, *Religion and Political Culture*, p. 43.

11. Gwandu, "Aspects of the Administration of Justice," p. 11.

12. Ibid.

13. Bello, "Muhammed Bello's Ideal of Criminal and Political Justice," p. 28.

14. Ibid., p. 29.

15. Gwandu, "Aspects of the Administration of Justice," pp. 13–15, 29–31.

16. Ibid., p. 12.

17. Ibid., p. 28.

18. Bello, "Muhammed Bello's Ideal of Criminal and Political Justice," p. 38.

19. Ibid., p. 39.

20. Paden, *Religion and Political Culture*, pp. 35–36.

21. See ibid., p. 36, for a discussion of overlapping identities in Kano city.

22. Ostein, *Study of the Court Systems*, p. 5.

23. Gwandu, "Aspects of the Administration of Justice," p. 16.

24. Ibid., p. 17.

25. Ibid., p. 19.

26. Ostein, *Study of the Court Systems*, p. 32.

27. Ibid., p. 9.

28. Cited ibid., p. 10.

29. Kumo, "Application of Islamic Law," p. 44.

30. Ibid., p. 45.

31. Ali, "Islamism," p. 12.

32. Ostein, *Study of the Court Systems*, pp. 6–7.

33. Ibid., p. 8.

34. Kilani, "Islam and Christian-Muslim Relations in Niger-Delta (Nigeria)," pp. 129–136.

35. Paden, *Religion and Political Culture*, p. 58.

36. Ibid., p. 57.

37. Ibid., p. 57.

38. "Zak Zaky Condemns US Attack on Afghanistan."

39. Paden, *Religion and Political Culture*, pp. 65–70.

40. Ibid., p. 70.
41. Yau, "Participation of Shiites," p. 4.
42. Ibid. For Sufism, see Paden, *Religion and Political Culture*, pp. 63–68.
43. Voll, "Fundamentalism in the Sunni Arab World," quoted in Ali, "Islamism," p. 11.
44. Yau, "Participation of Shiites," p. 5.
45. Ibid., p. 3.
46. Miles, "Religious Pluralisms," p. 220.
47. Quoted in Yau, "Participation of Shiites," p. 7.
48. Ibid., p. 33.
49. Ibid., p. 24.
50. Ibid., p. 5.
51. Ibid., p. 4.
52. Ibid., p. 7.
53. Ibid., pp. 3–4.
54. Quoted Ibid., p. 7.
55. Madugba, "Zak Zaky, Toro Oppose Sani on Sharia."
56. Yau, "Participation of Shiites," pp. 34–35.
57. Tahir, *The Last Imam*, p. 102–108.
58. *Crystal*, April 2000.
59. Yau, "Participation of Shiites," p. 7.
60. Ibid., pp. 7–9.
61. Kilani, "Islam and Christian-Muslim," p. 136.
62. Yau, "Participation of Shiites," p. 4.
63. "Nigeria: More than 100 Reportedly Die in Muslim-Christian Clashes in Kano."
64. "Nigeria Responds to Terror Attack Against New York and Washington," Anglican Communion News Service, September 19, 2001.
65. Ostein, *Study of the Court Systems*, p. 61.
66. *Crystal*, September 1999; *This Day*, April 26, 2000.
67. Byang, quoted in Ostein, *Study of the Court Systems*, p. 61; Yau, "Participation of Shiites," p. 7.
68. Sulaiman, "The *Sharia* and the 1979 Constitution," p. 53.
69. Ostein, *Study of the Court Systems*, pp. 55–58.
70. Sulaiman, "The *Sharia* and the 1979 Constitution," p. 53.
71. *This Day*, April 25, 2000.
72. *Sunday Vanguard*, April 2, 2000.
73. *Post Express*, April 27, 2000.
74. Essien, quoted in Ostein, *Study of the Court Systems*, p. 25; see "Criminal Law and Hudud Punishments," ibid., p. 69.
75. Ibid., p. 23.
76. Ibid., p. 38, Rashid, *Islamic Law*, p. 2.
77. Rashid, *Islamic Law*, p. 3.
78. Quoted in Ostein, *Study of the Court Systems*, p. 29.
79. Sulaiman, "The *Sharia* and the 1979 Constitution," pp. 52–53.

80. Ibid., p. 54.
81. Ostein, *Study of the Court Systems*, p. 56.
82. Ibid., p. 57.
83. Ibid., p. 58.
84. Quoted in Ali, "Islamism," p. 13.
85. Yau, "Participation of Shiites," p. 4.
86. "Frankly Speaking," Dele Sobowale, *Sunday Vanguard*, April 2, 2000.
87. *Tell*, May 1, 2000.
88. *News*, April 13, 2000, pp. 12–18.
89. Ali, "Islamism," p. 25; emphasis in original.
90. Oral interview, Frederick Quinn, Abuja, May 20, 2000.
91. Oral interview, Mukhtari Shitu, Abuja, December 5, 1996.
92. Ali, "Islamism," p. 13.
93. *Vanguard*, April 24, 2000.
94. Ibid.,
95. The list of Middle Belt states—with larger percentages of Christian populations than in the far North—differ but usually include Kwara, Plateau, Nasarawa, Niger, Kogi, Benue, and the Federal Capital Territory. *Guardian*, April 23, 2000.
96. Ibid.
97. *Tell*, May 1, 2000.
98. Oral interview, Mukhtari Shitu, April 20, 2000.
99. *This Day*, April 25, 2000.
100. *Guardian*, March 30, 2000.
101. *This Day*, April 25, 2000.
102. Miles, *Religious Pluralisms*, p. 220.
103. *Post Express*, April 27, 2000.
104. Ostein, *Study of the Court Systems*, p. 1.
105. Ibid.
106. Yau, "Participation of Shiites," p. 9.

Chapter 2

1. Voll, "Eastern Sudan," p. 153.
2. Peter K. Bechtold lists 597 tribes, speaking more than 400 languages, in "More Turbulence in Sudan, a New Politics This Time?," p. 1.
3. Holt and Daly, *History of the Sudan*, p. 2.
4. Memorandum, John O. Voll to Frederick Quinn, October 11, 2001.
5. Voll, "Eastern Sudan," p. 160.
6. Holt and Daly, *History of the Sudan*, p. 47.
7. Ibid., p. 76. A catalogue of the Mahdi's voluminous writings in Arabic is contained in O'Fahey and Bjørkelo, "Writings of Muhammad Abu Salim."
8. Voll, "Eastern Sudan," p. 155.
9. Holt and Daly, *History of the Sudan*, p. 78.
10. Ibid., p. 83.

11. Ibid., p. 105.

12. Ibid., p. 106.

13. Ibid., p. 107.

14. Voll, "Eastern Sudan," pp. 155, 158.

15. Holt and Daly, *History of the Sudan*, p. 107.

16. Ibid., p. 108.

17. Ibid., p. 111.

18. Ibid., pp. 115–116.

19. Ibid., pp. 123–125.

20. Voll, "Eastern Sudan," pp. 159–160.

21. Sidahmed, *Politics and Islam*, p. 1.

22. Ibid., p. 2.

23. Ibid., pp. 102–103.

24. Given to sweeping public gestures, Numayri marked the promulgation of the September Laws by dumping thousands of bottles of alcoholic beverages in the Nile. In the following year he abolished interest payments and income and other taxes, while instituting the traditional Islamic *zakat* as a source of government revenue. Warburg, "Sharia in Sudan."

25. Sidahmed, *Politics and Islam*, pp. 132–133.

26. Fluehr-Lobban, "Islamization in Sudan."

27. Sidahmed, *Politics and Islam*, pp. 136–137.

28. Ibid., pp. 122–123, 136–137; Simone, *In Whose Image?*, pp. 180–181.

29. To the charge of state support for terrorism, Bashir replies that "opening borders to all Muslims [is] not abetting terrorism." Petterson, *Inside Sudan*, p. 43.

30. Sidahmed, *Politics and Islam*, pp. 172–176.

31. Holt and Daly, *History of the Sudan*, p. 194.

32. Sidahmed, *Politics and Islam*, p. 225.

33. O'Fahey, "Islamic Hegemonies," p. 34.

34. Bechtold, "More Turbulence in Sudan," p. 12.

35. France is an exception, having maintained good relations with Sudan throughout the 1990s—officially, to protect its interests in Djibouti and francophone Africa, and unofficially, for commercial profit.

36. Petterson, *Inside Sudan*, p. 56.

37. Ibid., p. 184.

38. Mark Huband, "US Cruise Missile Attack May Have Upset a Shift of Sudan's Government," *Financial Times*, September 8, 1998, p. 7; BBC, Focus on Africa, April/June 1999, pp. 8–9.

39. Petterson, *Inside Sudan*, p. 95. Khartoum nevertheless continues to host rebel groups, such as the Eritrean Islamic Jihad, that are fighting elsewhere in the region.

40. Barton Gellman, "Sudan's Offer to Arrest Militant Fell Through After Saudis Said No," *Washington Post*, October 3, 2001, p. 1: "More than 35 Islamic Opponents Arrested in Sudan."

41. Huband, "US Cruise Missile Attack," p. 7.

42. Esposito and Voll, *Makers of Contemporary Islam*, pp. 118–149.

43. Boadansky, *Bin Laden, the Man Who Declared War on America*, pp. 32–36, 123–131, 205–206, 242–243, 297.

44. Petterson, *Inside Sudan*, p. 179.

45. El-Affendi, *Turabi's Revolution*, pp. 173–174.

46. Sidahmed, *Politics and Islam*, pp. 214–215.

47. Ibid., p. 128.

48. Simone, *In Whose Image?*, p. 189.

49. Ibrahim, "Theology of Modernity."

50. By 2001, oil revenues had doubled Sudan's defense budget as 2 million barrels a day were pumped from the fields, mostly in Sudan's South. "The fighting follows the oil," an observer stated. *Toronto Star*, June 17, 2001, B3.

51. Petterson, *Inside Sudan*, p. 111.

52. Memorandum, John O. Voll to Frederick Quinn, October 11, 2001.

53. Philip Smucker, "Islamic Leader's Support Grows While in Prison," *Houston Chronicle*, March 15, 2001.

54. Mohamed Osman, "Sudan Drops Case."

55. (Abu Dhabi) *Al-Itjihad*, July 17, 1998 (FBIS).

56. Mahamoud, "Sufism and Islamism in the Sudan."

57. General Numayri's military background and hegemonic political drive shaped the harsh application of the Sharia referred to as the September Laws. Although criticized by many Muslims and non-Muslims alike, they remain a stumbling block to unity in Sudan. They include a ban on alcohol, punishment by amputation for simple theft, whipping for other offenses, and other regressive features.

58. Voll, "Eastern Sudan," p. 165.

59. Karl Vick, "Sudan Wrestles with Its Pariah Image: War-Torn Nation Seen by Some as Complex Portrait," *Washington Post*, May 19, 2001, p. A 16.

60. Voll, Preface, *Sudan*, pp. vii–viii; Simone, *In Whose Image?*, p. 80.

Chapter 3

1. The Sufi brotherhoods are mystical Islamic orders that revere saintly founders and are politically active in sub-Saharan Africa.

2. Quoted in C. A. Quinn, *Mandingo Kingdoms*, p. 153.

3. Robinson, "Revolutions," p. 144.

4. Levtzion, "Islam in the Bilad al-Sudan," p. 68.

5. Ibid., p. 77.

6. Quoted in Oliver and Fage, *Short History of Africa*, p. 90.

7. Sanneh, *Crown and Turban*, p. 22.

8. Cheikh Anta Mbacke Babou, letter to Frederick Quinn, September 5, 2001.

9. C. A. Quinn, *Mandingo Kingdoms*, pp. 178–181.

10. Ibid., pp. 111–120.

11. Robinson, *Paths of Accommodation*; Klein, *Islam and Imperialism*; Levtzion and Pouwels, *History of Islam in Africa*.

12. Gellar, *Senegal*, p. 14.

13. O'Brien, Dunn, and Rathbone, *Contemporary West African States*, p. 161.
14. Hecht, "New York Dispatch."
15. Villalón, *Islamic Society*, pp. 67–68.
16. Robinson, *Paths of Accommodation*, pp. 75–96.
17. Quoted ibid., p. 89.
18. F. Quinn, *French Overseas Empire*, pp. 219–224.
19. Soudan, "L'Enquéte," pp. 20–29.
20. Roberts and Roberts, "Paintings Like Prayers," pp. 76–94.
21. "Information Minister Explains Iranian Embassy Closure."
22. "Niass's Release."
23. *Jeune Afrique l'intelligent*, p. 37.
24. Cheikh Anta Mbacke Babou to Frederick Quinn, email communication, August 16, 2001.
25. Country Report, Senegal.
26. Cheikh Anta Mbacke Babou, letter to Frederick Quinn, September 5, 2001.
27. Ibid.
28. Oral interview, Cheikh Anta Mbacke Babou, East Lansing, Michigan, May 30, 2001.
29. Clark, "Imperialism," pp. 149–167.
30. "President Urges Creation of African Anti-terrorism Pact."

Chapter 4

1. Swahili comes from the Arabic word *sahil*, meaning "coast."
2. Bonner, "A Reporter at Large." pp. 93–105.
3. Pouwels, "East African Coast," pp. 258–261.
4. Ibid., pp. 262–263.
5. Oded, *Islam and Politics*, p. 2.
6. Cooper, *Plantation Slavery*, p. 46.
7. Romero, *Lamu*, pp. 126–128.
8. Sperling, "Coastal Hinterland," p. 281.
9. O'Brien, "Coping with the Christians," p. 203.
10. Nimtz, *Islam and Politics*, p. 70.
11. Sperling, "Coastal Hinterland," pp. 288–289.
12. Oded, *Islam and Politics*, p. 3.
13. O'Brien, "Coping with the Christians," p. 204.
14. Sperling, "Coastal Hinterland," pp. 296–297.
15. Ibid., p. 296.
16. Oded, *Islam and Politics*, pp. 63–65.
17. Ibid., pp. 4–5.
18. Ibid., p. 15.
19. Ibid., pp. 139–140.
20. "Hundreds of Somalis Questioned in Police Swoop." (Nairobi) *Sunday Standard*, May 21, 1989 (FBIS text).

21. Odongo Oboyo and David Ochami, "Fanatics Terror on Bar Owners," (Nairobi) *Sunday Times*, February 13, 1997, p. 1.

22. Quoted in Kindy, *Life and Politics in Mombasa*, p. x.

23. Oded, *Islam and Politics*, p. 1.

24. "Islam Seen Increasing Adherents by Year 2000."

25. Oded, *Islam and Politics*, p. 16.

26. Ibid., p. 17.

27. Sperling, "Rural *Madrasas* of the Southern Kenya Coast," p. 209.

28. Oded, *Islam and Politics*, p. 16.

29. Ibid., p. 18.

30. O'Brien, "Coping with the Christians," pp. 204–205.

31. Ibid., p. 211.

32. "Local Shops Steer Clear of Satanic Author," (Nairobi) *Times*, February 21, 1989, p. 1. (FBIS text).

33. Chande, "Radicalism and Reform," pp. 350–351.

34. Oded, *Islam and Politics*, p. 49.

35. Ibid., p. 50.

36. Ibid., p. 54.

37. Ibid., pp. 67–68.

38. "Nassir Under Fire from Muslim Union," (Nairobi) *Daily News*, December 19, 1987, p. 5.

39. Oded, *Islam and Politics*, pp. 70–71.

40. Ibid., pp. 22–26.

41. Constantin, "Muslims and Politics," p. 20.

42. Oded, *Islam and Politics*, p. 23.

43. Ibid., p. 25.

44. Ibid., p. 24.

45. "Attorney General Rejects IPK Appeal to Register," Nairobi television in English, June 19, 1992 (FBIS Text).

46. Oded, *Islam and Politics*, pp. 142–143.

47. Stephen Buckley, "Tribal Tensions Explode in Carnage in Kenyan City." *Washington Post*, World News, August 20, 1997.

48. Oded, *Islam and Politics*, p. 11.

49. Throup, " 'Render Unto Caesar the Things That Are Caesar's.' "

50. Oded, *Islam and Politics*, pp. 102–103.

51. Ibid., p. 107.

52. "Muslim/Christian Tensions in Kenya on the Rise."

53. Blomfield, "Muslim and Christian Youths Clash in Kenyan Capital."

54. "Kenya: Anglican Primates Protest over Police Violence."

55. Oded, *Islam and Politics*, p. 16.

56. Chande, "Radicalism and Reform," p. 351.

57. Oded, *Islam and Politics*, p. 4.

58. "Proposals Adopted at the Meeting of Muslims."

59. "Kenya on a Tightrope," *Africa News*, December 21, 1987.

60. Arye Oded to Frederick Quinn, email communication, September 22, 2001.

61. "Suicide Bomber Survived to Name Others," *Washington Post*, November 23, 1998, A 18.

62. Oded, *Islam and Politics*, p. 83.

63. Chande, "Radicalism and Reform," p. 353.

64. Karl Vick, "Kenyans Know America's Pain." Support for Islamic Militancy Also Voiced at Site of '98 Attack," *Washington Post* (online), September 12, 2001.

65. "Muslims Take to the Streets Over Military Action," (Nairobi) *The Nation*, October 13, 2001.

66. Oded, *Islam and Politics*, pp. 149–150; *Shaikh* in Arabic is an honorific title, variously meaning chief, counselor, or leader. It is spelled different ways in different anglophone and francophone sources and has sometimes become part of a person's name. *Shakyh, Cheikh, Shaikh,* and *Sheikh* are all used in this work, according to the way people used the titles or spelled their names.

67. Ibid.

68. Ibid., p. 158.

69. Ibid., p. 154. "Islamic Party Leader Threatens to Eliminate Moi," BBC World Service in English, August 27, 1994 (FBIS-AFR-94-173, September 7, 1994), p. 7.

70. Oded, *Islam and Politics*, p. 43.

71. Ibid., p. 161.

72. "Kenya Says exiled Muslim Preacher Free to Return," Reuter, Nairobi, July 3, 1997.

73. Oded, *Islam and Politics*, p. 162.

74. Nairobi KNA in English, December 24, 1997 (FBIS text).

75. Arye Oded to Frederick Quinn, email communication, September 22, 2001.

76. Kasozi, "Christian-Muslim Inputs," p. 231.

77. Ibid., pp. 234–236.

78. Oded, *Islam and Politics*, pp. 90–91.

79. "President Moi Thanks Muslims for Loyalty," Nairobi domestic radio service in English, August 30, 1900 (FBIS text).

80. Oded, *Islam and Politics*, p. 93.

Chapter 5

1. Tayob, *Islamic Resurgence*, p. 39.

2. Ross, *Concise History of South Africa*, p. 3.

3. Shell, "Islam in Southern Africa," p. 327.

4. Latif, "Islam in South Africa."

5. Ross, *Concise History of South Africa*, p. 36.

6. Shell, "Islam in Southern Africa," pp. 327–328; Tayob, *Islamic Resurgence*, p. 39.

7. Shell, "Islam in Southern Africa," p. 330.

8. Quoted ibid.

9. Ibid., p. 338.

10. Ibid., p. 328.

11. Ibid., p. 329.

12. Abdulkader Tayob to Frederick Quinn, email communication, October 14, 2001.

13. Shell, "Islam in Southern Africa," p. 329.

14. Ibid., p. 330.

15. Quoted ibid., p. 329.

16. Shell, "Islam in Southern Africa," p. 330.

17. Quoted ibid., p. 331.

18. Ibid., pp. 333–334.

19. Tayob, *Islamic Resurgence*, p. 45.

20. Ibid.

21. Ibid., p. 41.

22. Ibid., p. 42.

23. Quoted in Chidester, Tobler, and Wratten, *Islam, Hinduism, and Judaism*, p. 4.

24. Shell, "Islam in Southern Africa," p. 332.

25. Ibid., pp. 338–339.

26. Ibid., p. 339.

27. Ibid., p. 340.

28. Ibid.

29. Ibid.

30. Voll, "Abduh and the Transvaal Fatwa," p. 27.

31. Tayob, *Islamic Resurgence*, p. 47.

32. Ibid., p. 78.

33. Shell, "Islam in Southern Africa," p. 342.

34. Abdulkader Tayob to Frederick Quinn, email communication, October 14, 2001.

35. "South Africa: Muslim Community Demands Apology from Botha," (Johannesburg) Agence France-Presse, October 31, 1986.

36. Tayob, *Islamic Resurgence*, p. 82.

37. "Islamic Association Supports Striking Hospital Workers." South African Press Association, Johannesburg, in English, July 13, 1992 (FBIS transcribed text).

38. Desai and Marney, *Killing of the Imam*, p. 1.

39. Ibid., p. 15.

40. "The Imam Spoke with Courage."

41. Haron, "The 'Muslim News.' " pp. 212–214, 220–221.

42. Tayob, *Islamic Resurgence*, pp. 83–87; Shell, "Islam in Southern Africa," p. 342.

43. Quoted in Tayob, *Islamic Resurgence*, p. 86.

44. Desai and Marney, *Killing of the Imam*, p. 1
45. Tayob, *Islamic Resurgence*, pp. 129–140.
46. Ibid., p. 94.
47. Ibid.
48. Ibid., pp. 102–103.
49. Ross, *Concise History of South Africa*, p. 161.
50. Tayob, *Islamic Resurgence*, p. 123.
51. Ibid., pp. 148–149.
52. Quoted ibid., p. 114.
53. Ibid., p. 126.
54. Argyle, "Muslims in South Africa," pp. 222–253.
55. "Islamic Religious Body Faces Major Split," (Durban) *Daily Times*, June 8, 1983, p. 15.
56. "Rushdie Must Repent, Say SA Muslims," (Johannesburg) *Weekly Mail*, February 24, 1989, p. 18.
57. "Muslim Community Speaks Out against Apartheid."
58. "Mandela Named Mahomed as First Post-Apartheid Chief Justice."
59. Shell, "Islam in Southern Africa," p. 343.
60. United Ulama Council of South Africa Press Statement, August 26, 1998.
61. Ross, *Concise History of South Africa*, p. 151.
62. "PAGAD Keeps Mum on US Attacks." *Cape Town*.
63. "The Days Ahead."
64. Ibid.
65. Watts, "Achmat Cassiem Interview"; M. Haron to Frederick Quinn, email communication, October 20, 2001.
66. "The PAGAD Connection." *Financial Mail*, August 16, 1996, p. 48.
67. Shell, "Islam in Southern Africa," p. 343.
68. "Vigilantes in South Africa Murder Suspected Drug Dealer."
69. Lynnette Johns, "PAGAD 'Plot.' Intended to Send Sinister Message to Magistrates," (Cape Town) *Cape Argus*, August 2, 2001.
70. U.S. Department of State, South Africa, Country Reports on Human Rights Practices 1998 and 2000.
71. Joint Press Release by the United Ulama Council of South Africa and the Media Review Network, September 18, 2000.
72. "One Solution, Islamic Revolution."
73. Meiring, "Militant Muslims Join the Fray."
74. National Public Radio news broadcast. WAMU, Washington, D.C., 6:30 A.M., October 15, 2001.
75. Watts, "Achmat Cassiem Interview."
76. Esack, *Qur'an, Liberation and Pluralism*.
77. Mahomed and Moosa, "Muslim Personal Law in the Context of Change."
78. Ebriham Moosa to Frederick Quinn, email communication, June 22, 2001.
79. Abdulkader Tayob to Frederick Quinn, email communication, October 14, 2001.

80. Esack, *On Being a Muslim*, pp. 173–174.
81. Esack, *Qur'an, Liberation and Pluralism*, p. 246.

Conclusion

1. Shaheen, *Reel Bad Arabs*, pp. 2–6.
2. Said, "Clash of Ignorance."

References

Adas, Michael, ed. *Islamic and European Expansion: The Forging of a Global Order.* Philadelphia: Temple University Press, 1993.

A Law to Establish Shari'a Courts in Zamfara State. October 8, 1999.

A Law to Establish a Sharia'ah Penal Code for Zamfara State. January 27, 2000.

Ali, Ameer. "Islamism: Emancipation, Protest and Identity." *Journal of Muslim Minority Affairs,* vol. 20, no. 1 (April 2000): 11–28.

Alpers, Edward A. "East Central Africa." In *The History of Islam in Africa,* ed. Nehemia Levtzion and Randall L. Pouwels. Athens: Ohio University Press, 2000.

Anderson, G. Norman. *Sudan in Crisis, The Failure of Democracy.* Gainesville: University Press of Florida, 1999.

Argyle, W. J. "Muslims in South Africa: Origins, Development and Present Economic Status." *Journal of Muslim Minority Affairs,* vol. 3, no. 2 (1981): 222–253.

Azumah, John Alembillah. *The Legacy of Arab-Islam in Africa.* Oxford: Oneworld, 2001.

Becktold, Peter K., "More Turbulence in Sudan: A New Politics This Time?" In *Sudan, State and Society in Crisis,* ed. John O. Voll. Bloomington: Indiana University Press, 1991.

Behrman, Lucy. *Muslim Brotherhoods and Politics in Senegal.* Cambridge, Mass.: Harvard University Press, 1970.

Bello, Omar. "Muhammad Bello's Ideal of Criminal and Political Justice." In *Islamic Law in Nigeria,* ed. Sayed Khalid Rashid. Lagos: Islamic Publications Bureau, 1986.

Boadansky, Yossef. *Bin Laden, the Man Who Declared War on America.* Roseville, Calif.: Prima Publishing, 2001.

Blomfield, Adrian. "Muslim and Christian Youths Clash in Kenyan Capital." Anglican Communion News Service, 2319, Kenya, December 4, 2000.

Bonner, Raymond. "A Reporter at Large: African Democracy." The New Yorker, September 3, 1990.

Bravmann, René. "Islamic Art and Material Culture in Africa." In The History of Islam in Africa, ed. Nehemia Levtzion and Randall L. Pouwells. Athens: Ohio University Press, 2000.

Chande, Abdin. "Radicalism and Reform in East Africa." In The History of Islam in Africa, ed. Nehemia Levtzion and Randall L. Pouwels. Athens: Ohio University Press, 2000.

Chidester, David, Judy Tobler, and Darrel Wratten. Islam, Hinduism, and Judaism in South Africa, an Annotated Bibliography. Westport, Conn.: Greenwood Press, 1997.

Clark, Andrew F. "Imperialism, Independence, and Islam in Senegal and Mali." Africa Today, vol. 46, no. 3 /4 (Summer/Autumn 1999).

Constantin, François. "Muslims and Politics: The Attempts to Create Muslim National Organizations in Tanzania, Uganda, and Kenya." In Religion and Politics in East Africa, ed. Holger Bernt Hansen and Michael Twaddle. London: James Currey, 1995.

Cooper, Frederick. Plantation Slavery on the East Coast of Africa. New Haven, Conn.: Yale University Press, 1977.

Coulon, Christian. "The Grand Magal in Touba: A religious Festival of the Mouride Brotherhood of Senegal." (London) African Affairs, vol. 98, no. 391 (April 1999).

Country Report, Senegal. (London) The Economist Intelligence Unit, June 2001.

Danbazau, Mallam Lawan. Politics and Religion in Nigeria. Toga Commercial Press, 1993.

Dangor, Suleman. "The Expression of Islam in South Africa." Journal of Muslim Minority Affairs, vol.17, no.1 (1997).

"The Days Ahead." FBIS transcribed text, FBIS Document ID: AFP20220210100000081, Entry Date 10/10/2001.

Desai, Barney, and Cardiff Marney. The Killing of the Imam: South African Tyranny Defied by Courage and Faith. Forward by Sir Dingle Goot QC. New York: Quartet Books, 1978.

El-Affendi, Abdelwahab. Turabi's Revolution: Islam and Power in Sudan. London: Grey Seal, 1991.

Entelis, John P., ed. Islam Democracy and the State in North Africa. Bloomington: Indiana University Press, 1997.

Esack, Farid. On Being a Muslim: Finding a Path in the World Today. Oxford: Oneworld, 2000.

———. Qur'an. Liberation and Pluralism, an Islamic Perspective of Interreligious Solidarity Against Oppression. Oxford: Oneworld, 1997.

Esposito, John L., and John O. Voll. Makers of Contemporary Islam. New York: Oxford University Press, 2001.

Fall, Elimane. "Sénégal du Commis de l'État." *Jeune Afrique Economique*, April 30–May 13, 2001.

Fluehr-Lobban, Carolyn. "Islamization in Sudan: A Critical Assessment." *Sudan, State and Society in Crisis*, ed. John O. Voll. Bloomington: Indiana University Press, 1991.

Gellar, Sheldon. *Senegal, an African Nation Between Islam and the West*. Boulder, Col.: Westview Press, 1982.

Gray, Christopher. "The Rise of the Niassne Tijaniya, 1875 to the Present." In *Islam et Islamismes au Sud du Sahara*, ed. Ousmane Kane and Jean-Louis Triaud. Paris: Éditions Karthala, 1998.

Gwandu, A. A. "Aspects of the Administration of Justice in the Sokoto Caliphate and Shaykh Abdullahi Ibn Fodio's Contribution to It." In *Islamic Law in Nigeria*, ed. Sayed Khalid Rashid. Lagos: Islamic Publications Bureau, 1986.

Hale, Sondra. *Gender Politics in Sudan: Islamism, Socialism, and the State*. Boulder, Col.: Westview Press, 1997.

Hansen, Holger Bernt, and Michael Twaddle, eds. *Religion and Politics in East Africa*. London: James Currey, 1995.

Haron, Muhammed. "The 'Muslim News': An Islamic Identity in South Africa." In *Muslim Identity and Social Change in Sub Saharan Africa*, ed. Louis Brenner. Bloomington: Indiana University Press, 1993.

Haron, Muhammed. *Muslims in South Africa, An Annotated Bibliography*. Cape Town: South African Library, in association with Centre for Contemporary Islam, UCT, 1997.

Harrison, Chris. *France and Islam in West Africa, 1860–1960*. Cambridge: Cambridge University Press, 1988.

Harrow, Kenneth W., ed. *Faces of Islam in African Literature*. Portsmouth, N.H.: Heinemann, 1991.

Harrow, Kenneth W. "Islamic Literature in Africa." In *The History of Islam in Africa*, ed. Nehemia Levtzion and Randall L. Pouwels. Athens: Ohio University Press, 2000.

Hecht, David. "New York Dispatch: Watch Men." *New Republic*, April 12, 1999.

Holt, P. M., and M. W. Daly. *A History of the Sudan from the Coming of Islam to the Present Day*. New York: Longman, Pearson Education, 2000.

Hunwick, John O., ed. *Religion and National Integration in Africa: Islam, Christianity and Politics in the Sudan and Nigeri*. Evanston, Ill.: Northwestern University Press, 1992.

Hunwick, John. "Sub-Saharan Africa and the Wider World of Islam." In *African Islam and Islam in Africa: Encounters Between Sufis and Islamists*, ed. David Westerlund and Eva Evers Rosander. Athens: Ohio University Press, 1997.

"The Imam Spoke with Courage." *Muslim Views*, vol. 1, no. 10 (October 1987): p. 11.

"Information Minister Explains Iranian Embassy Closure." FBIS text, ABO82240. Agence France-Presse text, in English, Paris, February 8, 1984.

Jeune Afrique l'intelligent. No. 2107, 5–11 Juin 2001.

Ibrahim, Abdullahi Ali. "A Theology of Modernity: Hasan Al-Turabi and Islamic Renewal in Sudan." *Africa Today*, vol. 46, nos. 3 and 4 (Summer/Autumn 1999).

Kasozi, A. B. K. "Christian-Muslim Inputs Into Public Policy Formation in Kenya, Tanzania and Uganda." In *Religion and Politics in East Africa*, ed. Holger Bernt Hansen and Michael Twaddle. London: James Currey, 1995.

"Kenya: Anglican Primates Protest over Police Violence." (Online: www.wfn.org/1997/07/msg00195.html).

Kilani, Abdul Razaq. "Islam and Christian-Muslim Relations in Niger-Delta." *Journal of Muslim Minority Affairs*, vol. 20, no. 1 (April 2000).

Kindy, Hyder. *Life and Politics in Mombasa*. Nairobi: East African Publishing House, 1972.

Klein, Martin. *Islam and Imperialism in Senegal: Sine-Saloum, 1847–1914*. Stanford, Calif.: Stanford University Press, 1968.

Kubi, Anne. "The Early Muslim Communities of Nairobi (Kenya)." *Islam et Sociétés au sud du Sahara*, vol. 6 (November 1992).

Kumo, Sulaiman. "The Application of Islamic Law in Northern Nigeria: Problems and Prospects." In *Islamic Law In Nigeria*. Sayed Khalid Rashid, ed. Lagos: Islamic Publications Bureau, 1986.

Latif, Abdul. "Islam In South Africa." (Online: www.themodernreligion.com/convert.html.)

Levtzion, Nehemia. "Islam in the Bilad al-Sudan to 1800." In *The History of Islam in Africa*, ed. Nehemia Levtzion and Randall L. Pouwels. Athens: Ohio University Press, 2000.

Levtzion, Nehemia, and Randall L. Pouwels, eds. *The History of Islam in Africa*. Athens: Ohio University Press, 2000.

Loimeier, Roman. *Islamic Reform and Political Change in Northern Nigeria*. Evanston, Ill.: Northwestern University Press, 1997.

Lubbe, Gerrie. "The Soweto *Fatwa*: A Muslim Response to a Watershed Event in South Africa." *Journal of Muslim Minority Affairs*, vol. 17, no. 2 (1997).

Maalouf, Amin. *The Crusades Through Arab Eyes*. Trans. Jon Rothchild. New York: Schocken Books, 1984.

Madugba, Agaju. "Zak Zaky, Toro Oppose Sani on Sharia." (Lagos) *Guardian*. (Rev. online, October 13, 1999: http://www.ihrc.org/countries/Nigeria/Interview2.htm.)

Magassouba, Moriba. *L'Islam au Sénégal, Demain les Mollahs?* Paris: Éditions Karthala, 1985.

Mahamoud, Muhammad. "Sufism and Islamism in the Sudan." In *African Islam and Islam in Africa: Encounters between Sufis and Islamists*, ed. Eva Evers Rosander and David Westerlund. Athens: Ohio University Press, 1997.

Mahida, Ebrahim Mahomed. *Islam in South Africa: Bibliography, Organizations, Periodicals and Population*. Durban: Centre for Research in Islamic Studies, University of Durban—Westville, 1995.

Mahomed, Ashraf, and Majma Moosa. "Muslim Personal Law in the Context of Change." (Online: www.uct.ac.za/depts/religion/law98.htm.)

"Mandela Named Mahomed as First Post-Apartheid Chief Justice." South African Press Association report, in English (FBIS transcribed text). Johannesburg, October 26, 1996.

Mandivenga, Ephraim. "The Role of Islam in Southern Africa." In *Religion and Politics in Southern Africa*, ed. Carl Fredrik Hallencreutz and Mai Palmberg. Uppsala: Scandinavian Institute of African Studies, 1991.

Manger, Leif, ed. *Muslim Diversity: Local Islam in Global Contexts*. London: Curzon, 1999.

Martin, B. G. *Muslim Brotherhoods in Nineteenth Century Africa*. Cambridge: Cambridge University Press, 1976.

Meiring, Desmond. "Militant Muslims Join the Fray." (Online: www.oneworld.org/ni/issue212update.htm.)

Miles, William F. S. "Religious Pluralisms in Northern Nigeria." In *The History of Islam in Africa*, ed. Nehemia Levtzion and Randall L. Pouwels. Athens: Ohio University Press, 2000.

Miller, Judith. *God Has Ninety-Nine Names*. New York: Simon and Schuster, 1996.

Moorehead, Alan. *The White Nile*. New York: Vantage Books, 1983.

"Muslim/Christian Tensions in Kenya on the Rise." U.S. State Department report. Nairobi 012638, August 28, 1998.

"Muslim Community Speaks Out AgainstApartheid." Interview with Muhammad Shir Shawddhari. (Tripoli) *Al-Da'wah Al-Islamiyah*, in Arabic (FBIS transcription), February 18, 1987.

Nelson, Harold D., ed. *Sudan: A Country Study, Foreign Area Studies, American University*. Washington, D.C.: U.S. Government Printing Office, 1982.

Neufeld, Charles. *A Prisoner of the Khaleefa*. New York: Putnam, 1899.

"Niass's Release." FBIS text, CSO: 4700/1098 E. Dakar, March 30, 1982.

"Nigeria: More than 100 Reportedly Die in Muslim-Christian Clashes in Kano." FBIS Document ID: AFP 20011013000081. BBC World Service in English 1706 GMT, London, October 13, 2001.

Nimtz, August H., Jr. *Islam and Politics in East Africa: The Sufi Order in Tanzania*. Minneapolis: University of Minnesota Press, 1980.

Njoroge, Lawrence M. *A Century of Catholic Endeavour: Holy Ghost and Consolata Missions in Kenya*. Nairobi: Pauline Publications of Africa, 1999.

O'Brien, Donal B. Cruise. "Coping with the Christians: The Muslim Predicament in Kenya." In *Religion and Politics in East Africa*, ed. Holger Bernt Hansen and Michael Twaddle. London: James Currey: 1995.

———. *The Mourides of Senegal: The Political and Economic Organization of an Islamic Brotherhood*. Oxford: Oxford University Press, 1971.

O'Brien, Donal B. Cruise, John Dunn, and Richard Rathbone, eds. *Contemporary West African States*. Cambridge: Cambridge University Press, 1989.

Oded, Arye. *Islam and Politics in Kenya*. Boulder, Col.: Lynne Rienner, 2000.

O'Fahey, R. S. "Islamic Hegemonies in the Sudan: Sufism, Mahdism, and Islamism." In *Muslim Identity and Social Change in Sub-Sahara Africa*, ed. Louis Brenner. Bloomington: Indiana University Press, 1993.

O'Fahey, R. S., and Anders Bjørkelo. "Writings of Muhammad Abu Salim." *Sudanic Africa*, vol. 1 (1990).

Oliver, Roland, and J. D. Fage. *A Short History of Africa*. Baltimore, Md.: Penguin Books, 1968.

"One Solution, Islamic Revolution." Supplement to *Muslim Views*, April 1990, Issued by Qibla-Cape.

Osman, Mohamed. "Sudan Drops Case Against Political Leader Hasan al-Turabi." Associated Press. (Rev. online October 1, 2001: http://www.sudan.net/news/posted/3526.html)

Ostein, Philip. *A Study of the Court Systems of Northern Nigeria with a Proposal for the Creation of Lower Sharia Courts in Some Northern States*. Jos: Centre for Development Studies, University of Jos, 1999.

Paden, John. *Ahmadu Bello Sardauna of Sokoto: Values and Leadership in Nigeria*. Zaria: Hudahuda Publishing Company, 1986.

————. *Religion and Political Culture in Kano*. Berkeley: University of California Press, 1973.

"PAGAD Keeps Mum on US Attacks." *Cape Town* (Rev. September 11, 2001. Online: http://iafrica.com/news/sa/801571.htm).

Pearson, M. N. "The Indian Ocean and the Red Sea." In *The History of Islam in Africa*, eds. Nehemia Levtzion and Randall L. Pouwels. Athens: Ohio University Press, 2000.

Petterson, Donald. *Inside Sudan: Political Islam, Conflict, and Catastrophe*. Boulder, Col.: Westview Press, 1998.

Pouwels, Randall L. "The East African Coast, c. 780 to 1900 C.E." In *The History of Islam in Africa*, ed. Nehemia Levtzion and Randall L. Pouwels. Athens: Ohio University Press, 2000.

————. *Horn and Crescent: Cultural Change and Traditional Islam on the East Africa Coast (800–1900)*. Cambridge: Cambridge University Press, 1987.

"President Urges Creation of African Anti-terrorism Pact." *UN Integrated Regional Information Network*. (Rev. online, September 21, 2001: http://allafrica.com/stories/200109210005.html.)

"Proposals Adopted at the Meeting of Muslims." FBIS report. MSETO in Swahili, Nairobi, May 9, 1981.

Quinn, Charlotte A. *Mandingo Kingdoms of the Senegambia*. Evanston, Ill.: Northwestern University Press, 1972.

Quinn, Frederick. *The French Overseas Empire*. Westport, Conn.: Praeger, 2000.

Rashid, Syed Khalid. *Islamic Law in Nigeria*. Lagos: Islamic Publications Bureau, 1986.

"*Report of the Committee Set Up to Advice [sic] the Sqokoto State Government on the Establishment of Sharia.*" October 13, 1999.

Roberts, Allen F., and Mary Nooter Roberts. " 'Paintings Like Prayers,' the Hidden Side of Senegalese Image-Glass Texts." *Research in African Literature*, vol. 31, no. 4 (Winter 2000).

Robinson, David. "France as a Muslim Power in West Africa." *Africa Today*, vol. 46, no. 3/4 (Summer/Autumn 1999).

————. *Paths of Accommodation: Muslim Societies and French Colonial Authorities in Senegal and Mauritania, 1880–1920.* Athens: Ohio University Press, 2000.

————. "Revolutions in the Western Sudan." In *The History of Islam in Africa*, ed. Nehemia Levtzion and Randall L. Pouwels. Athens: Ohio University Press, 2000.

Robinson, David, and Jean-Louis Triaud, eds. *Le temps des marabouts: Itinéraires et stratégies islamiques en Afrique occidentale française v. 1880–1960.* Paris: Éditions Karthala, 1998.

Romero, Patricia W. *Lamu: History, Society and Family in an East African Port City.* Princeton, N.J.: Markus Wiener, 1997.

Rosander, Eva Evers, and David Westerlund, eds. *African Islam and Islam in Africa: Encounters Between Sufis and Islamists.* Athens: Ohio University Press, 2000.

Ross, Robert. *A Concise History of South Africa.* Cambridge: Cambridge University Press, 1999.

Said, Edward W. "Clash of Ignorance." *The Nation*, October 22, 2001.

Sanneh, Lamin. *The Crown and the Turban: Muslims and West African Pluralism.* Boulder, Col.: Westview Press, 1997.

Shaheen, Jack G. *Reel Bad Arabs.* New York: Olive Branch Press, 2001.

Shell, Robert C.-H. "Islam in Southern Africa, 1652–1998." In *The History of Islam in Africa*, ed. Nehemia Levtzion and Randall L. Pouwels. Athens: Ohio University Press, 2000.

Sidahmed, Abdel Salam. *Politics and Islam in Contemporary Sudan.* New York: St. Martin's Press, 1996.

Simone, T. Abdou Maliqalim. *In Whose Image? Political Islam and Urban Practices in Sudan.* Chicago: University of Chicago Press, 1994.

Slatin, Sir Rudolf Carl. *Fire and Sword in the Sudan, 1879–1895.* Trans. Maj. F. Wingate. London: E. Arnold, 1896.

Soudan, François. "L'Enquéte, La France Láche L'Afrique." *Jeune Afrique L'Intelligent*, no. 2098 (March 27–April 2, 2001).

Sperling, David C. "Rural *Madrasas* of the Southern Kenya Coast, 1971–92." In *Muslim Identity and Social Change in Sub-Saharan Africa.* Ed. Louis Brenner. Bloomington: Indiana University Press, 1993.

Sperling, David C., with additional material by Jose H. Kagabo. "The Coastal Hinterland and Interior of East Africa." In *The History of Islam in Africa*, ed. Nehemia Levtzion and Randall L. Pouwels. Athens: Ohio University Press, 2000.

Sulaiman, Ibrahim K. R. "The *Sharia* and the 1979 Constitution." In *Islamic Law in Nigeria*, ed. Sayed Khalid Rashid. Lagos: Islamic Publications Bureau, 1986.

Tahir, Ibrahim. *The Last Imam.* London: KPI, 1984.

Tayob, Abdulkader. *Islamic Resurgence in South Africa: The Muslim Youth Movement.* Cape Town: University of Cape Town, 1995.

————. *Islam in South Africa, Mosques, Imams and Sermons.* Gainesville: University Press of Florida, 1999.

Throup, David. " 'Render Unto Caesar the Things That Are Caesar's.' The Politics of Church-State Conflict in Kenya, 1978–1990." In *Religion and Politics in*

East Africa: The Period Since Independence, ed. Holger Bernt Hansen and Michael Twaddle. Athens: Ohio University Press, 1995.

Usman, Yusufu Bala. *The Manipulation of Religion in Nigeria: 1977–1987*. Kaduna: Vanguard Printers, 1987.

Vahed, Goolam. "Changing Islamic Traditions and Emerging Identities in South Africa." *Journal of Muslim Minority Affairs*, vol. 20, no.1 (2000): 43–73.

"Vigilantes in South Africa Murder Suspected Drug Dealer in Fight against Gangs and Drugs." *International News Briefs* (Rev. September 1996. Online: http://www.ndsn.org/SEPT96/PAGAD.html, September 13, 2001).

Villalón, Leonardo A. *Islamic Society and State Power in Senegal: Disciples and Citizens in Fatick*. Cambridge: Cambridge University Press, 1995.

Voll, John O. "Abduh and the Transvaal Fatwa: The Neglected Question." In *Islam and the Question of Minorities*, ed. Tamara Sonn, pp. 27–39. Tampa: University of South Florida/Scholars Press, 1996.

———. "The Eastern Sudan, 1822 to the Present." In *The History of Islam in Africa*, ed. Nehemia Levtzion and Randall L. Pouwels. Athens: Ohio University Press, 2000.

———. "Islam in Africa: Frameworks" (working paper). Georgetown University, Washington, D.C., 2001.

———. "Islam as a Special World-System." *Journal of World History*, vol. 5, no. 2 (1994): 213–226.

———, ed. *Sudan: State and Society in Crisis*. Bloomington: Indiana University Press, 1991.

———. "Sultans, Saints, and Presidents: The Islamic Community and the State in North Africa." In *Democracy and the State in North Africa*, ed. John P. Entelis. Bloomington: Indiana University Press, 1997.

Von Sievers, Peter. "Patterns of Islamization and Varieties of Religious Experience Among Muslims of Africa." In *The History of Islam in Africa*, ed. Nehemia Levtzion and Randall L. Pouwells. Athens: Ohio University Press, 2000.

Wall, James M. "Reel Bad Arabs." *Christian Century*, vol. 118, no. 22 (August 1–8, 2001).

Warburg, Gabriel R. "The Sharia in Sudan: Implementation and Repercussions." In *Sudan: State and Society in Crisis*, ed. John O. Voll. Bloomington: Indiana University Press, 1991.

Watts, Derek. "Achmat Cassiem Interview," September 28, 2001 (Online: www:Chretiens-et-juifs.org/JIHAD/Cassiem_Interview.htm.)

Yau, Y. Z. "The Participation of Shiites and Almajirai in Religious Conflicts in Northern Nigeria." *Equal Justice*, March–May, 1999, pp. 3–9.

"Zak Zaky Condemns US Attack on Afghanistan." (Abuja) *Daily Trust*. (Rev. online, October 12, 2001: http://allafrica.com/stories/200110120032.html.)

Oral Interviews by the Authors

Babou, Cheikh Anta Mbacke, May 30, 2001, East Lansing, Michigan.
Birniwa, Musa Muhammad, April 27, 2000; May 4, 2000; May 16, 2000; and May
    18, 2000; Abuja, Nigeria.
Moss, Mitchell, April 19, 2000, Abuja, Nigeria.
Shitu, Mukhtari, December 5, 1996; March 28, 2000; and April 20, 2000; Abuja,
    Nigeria.
Yariman, Governor Alhaji Sani Ahmad, May 9, 2000, Abuja, Nigeria.

Index

Abacha, General Sani, 9, 13, 25, 28, 43–44, 46–47, 56, 61–62
Aga Kahn, and Shiite Ismailis (Kenya), 113, 117, 127, 153n41, 153n44, 153n47, 153n56, 153n59, 153n62, 154n85, 154n106
Almajiranci educational system (Nigeria), 48
Almoravid conquest, 19–20, 91–92
American embassy bombing (Kenya), 27, 81, 121–122, 125, 149
Ansar, 15, 69, 71
Arabic, 8–9, 18, 23, 42, 67–68, 71, 74, 78, 93, 131, 135, 137, 145, 154n7, 157n1, 159n66

Balala, Shaik Khalid, 120, 122–123
Bamba, Amadou, 10, 96, 98, 101, 104
Bashir, President Omar Hassan (Sudan), 76–80, 84–86
Bin Laden, Osama, 4, 29, 43, 77, 80–82, 121–122, 156n43
British colonial rule, 39–40, 53, 112

Casamance region of Senegal, 30, 100
Cassiem, Achmet, 161n65, 161n75

Christianity, 3–6, 9–15, 21, 26, 28, 30, 32, 34, 38, 41, 48–56, 60, 62–71, 94, 100–101, 109–111, 113–116, 118–121, 124–125, 127, 129–130, 132–133, 135–136, 147–148, 150, 154n95, 157n9, 158n30, 158n52, 158n53
Claremont Road Mosque (South Africa), 23, 25, 135–136, 145
Crusades, 4–5, 87, 151n3

Diouf, President Abdou (Senegal), 98, 100, 102, 105

Esack, Moulana Farid, 25, 145–146, 161n76, 162n80, 162n81
Ethiopia, 6, 21–22, 81–82

Female genital mutilation, 25, 83, 112
French colonial rule, 93–95

Ghana, 18–19, 91
Gordon, Charles, 69
Gumi, Abubakar, 26, 28, 42–43, 61